painted TREASURES

Projects and Inspiration from Today's Best Decorative Painters

Elizabeth M. Burd

2007

NORTH LIGHT BOOKS
CINCINNATI, OHIO
www.artistsnetwork.com

DECORATIVE ARTS COLLECTION, INC.

fw

F+W PUBLICATIONS, INC.

Published by North Light Books, an imprint of F+W Publications, Inc., 4700 East
Galbraith Road, Cincinnati, Ohio, 45236. (800) 289-0963. First Edition.

Other fine North Light Books are available from your local bookstore, art supply
store or direct from the publisher.

11 10 09 08 07   5 4 3 2 1

Distributed in Canada by Fraser Direct
100 Armstrong Avenue
Georgetown, ON, Canada L7G 5S4
Tel: (905) 877-4411

Distributed in the U.K. and Europe by David & Charles
Brunel House, Newton Abbot, Devon, TQ12 4PU, England
Tel: (+44) 1626 323200, Fax: (+44) 1626 323319
Email: postmaster@davidandcharles.co.uk

Distributed in Australia by Capricorn Link
P.O. Box 704, S. Windsor NSW, 2756 Australia
Tel: (02) 4577-3555

Library of Congress Cataloging-in-Publication Data

Painted treasures : projects and inspiration from today's best decorative painters /
Decorative Arts Collection, Inc.
        p. cm.
    Includes index.
    ISBN-13: 978-1-58180-880-3 (hardcover : alk. paper)
    ISBN-10: 1-58180-880-1 (hardcover : alk. paper)
    1. Painting--Technique.   2. Decoration and ornament. I. Decorative Arts Collection.
TT385.P364 2007
745.7'23--dc22
                            2006030130

Edited by Andy B. Jones and Kathy Kipp
Designed by Clare Finney
Production coordinated by Greg Nock

METRIC CONVERSION CHART

TO CONVERT	TO	MULTIPLY BY
Inches	Centimeters	2.54
Centimeters	Inches	0.4
Feet	Centimeters	30.5
Centimeters	Feet	0.03
Yards	Meters	0.9
Meters	Yards	1.1

DEDICATION

"This book and the paintings it contains is dedicated to all those whose works have inspired us through the years, and to those who will be inspired in the future by the works we create."

Director, Decorative Arts Collection Museum
   Andy B. Jones

table of contents

95 beautiful full-color photos of selected treasures from the Decorative Arts Collection, including significant pieces from the founders and pioneers of decorative painting such as Peter Ompir, Peter Hunt, Joan Johnson and Priscilla Hauser.

introduction

A BRIEF HISTORY OF THE DECORATIVE ARTS COLLECTION

In October of 1972, Priscilla Hauser gathered 22 decorative painters in Tulsa, Oklahoma, to discuss the formation of an organization of decorative painters. Even from this early time the dream of a museum was present. A committee to discuss the formation of a museum was established. This committee was to meet in Lenexa, Kansas, the following year.

As the Society of Decorative Painters began to grow, publication began on *The Decorative Painter* magazine. Editor Emeritus, Mary Jo Leisure, began to ask artists to donate works. Contributors to the magazine not only donated their work, but were honored to be asked to do so. Such is the love painters have for the art form and the preservation of it.

For the next several years, artwork continued to be donated and committees met to discuss the museum. Since this committee had no budget, forward movement on a museum moved at a snail's pace. That is, until 1979.

In 1979 five of the committee members traveled to Decorah, Iowa, to visit the Norwegian American Museum and to consult with Dr. Marion Nelson, museum director and Chairman of the Department of Art at the University of Minnesota. His advice: don't worry about the location of a museum. Collect. Collect. Collect.

It was obvious the time had come to form a corporation separate from the Society that could receive contributions, both monetary and works of art, which would be tax deductible. Accordingly, legal procedures began in 1981 for this new organization, but it was to be more than a year before Mary Lou Garrison, then president of the Society of Decorative Painters, signed the Articles of Incorporation.

One of the first decisions required was the choice of a name for this corporation. After much discussion, eleven different names were suggested. "The Decorative Arts Collection, Inc." was ultimately selected as the title for this infant organization. The title told what we were and what we intended to do. And when the corporation finally received its IRS confirmation, the Society of Decorative Painters transferred ownership of all pieces in the fledgling collection, together with the entire library of hundreds of publications by members of the Society, to the ownership of the new DAC, barely eleven years after the genesis of the Society of Decorative Painters.

Although the new bylaws envisioned a day when the Decorative Arts Collection would be governed by a separate board, for the first years, the board of the DAC and the board of the Society of Decorative Painters consisted of the same people.

However, taking Dr. Nelson's advice to heart, when the Board of Trustees was informed that a significant, authenticated piece of American Country painted tinware, a gooseneck coffeepot circa late 1700s, was going to be available at auction, the board of directors authorized a representative to bid several thousand dollars for the piece. Bidding against buyers from the entire country, the coffeepot became the proud possession of the Decorative Arts Collection and was to become the signature piece for the DAC.

Shortly after this acquisition, we were informed of some Peter Ompir painted pieces available for purchase. With the help of the Heart of Ohio Tole Chapter, this purchase of the Ompir pieces was made possible. Next, with the acquisition of a large cupboard painted by Peter Hunt, the DAC now included significant works by two of the artists most responsible for the revival of decorative painting in the first half of the twentieth century, as well as the coffeepot, an eighteenth century treasure. The vision was becoming a reality.

Now that the DAC was a separate entity, the "Museum Committee" became the "Decorative Arts Collection Committee," and later was named the

The plate is inscribed: *Decorative Arts Collection* ♥ 2007, 1982, 25th *Anniversary*

"Acquisitions Committee." At its first meeting in 1983, as ideas and plans were percolating for the DAC's future, someone mentioned that we needed a logo. Joan Johnson, a member of that first committee, turned over a page of "doodles" she'd been sketching and said, "Like this?" There was a page full of variations on the letters DAC superimposed on a stylized heart that was to identify the Decorative Arts Collection, Inc. for the next 25 years.

Another recommendation of that committee was the inauguration of a juried competition to help bring the best in contemporary works of art into the collection through purchase awards funded by industry sponsors. The first awards were presented in 1984 in Albuquerque, New Mexico, with two judges from the art world outside of decorative painting as well as one from within. Through the years, the juried competition has become a vehicle for transitioning from a collection focused on representative works of American artists that included our diverse ethnic origins, to award winners from countries throughout the world who paint in a wide variety of styles. In 2005 winners hailed from Argentina, Australia, Japan, and the United States.

Although the Society of Decorative Painters has always been extremely generous in their support, the opportunity to acquire more pieces of significant historical importance and to have funds to allow for separate DAC activities became a reality with the innovation of the "Friends" program in 1999. At long last, the DAC could elect a separate board, denominated "Trustees" because they truly considered the collection a trust they were to guard and enhance. Thus they could turn their attention to this single goal with the authority to pursue acquisitions, present special educational forums, and to plan for the maintenance and display of the collection in rented space within the building housing the Society of Decorative Painters in Wichita, Kansas. Cooperation with the Wichita Museum community, tours of the exhibit space, and new educational activities could be added as well as expanded convention opportunities for lectures, seminars, the jurying of the Decorative Arts Collection Awards, managing a consignment sale of selected artists' pieces, and showcasing pieces from the collection.

In 2003 the DAC mounted its first traveling exhibition, titled "The Fathers of American Decorative Painting," featuring works of our antecedents, Peter Hunt, Per Lysne, and Peter Ompir. In 2004, an exhibition titled "A Sentimental Collection of Roses" was launched. This exhibition featured 74 new rose paintings created specifically for it. A companion book to the exhibition was a runaway hit!

This book led to the DAC's first overseas exhibition. The entire "Rose Collection," together with 71 other pieces from the collection, was sent on a nine month tour of Japan, with the cost underwritten by Nihon Vogue Company. The collection was viewed by more than 100,000 enthusiasts in seven different cities.

In 2006 the DAC hired its first Museum Director, Andy B. Jones, a major step leading to far-seeing plans for future outreach into the art world beyond the decorative painting industry. In 2007, its 25th year, the Decorative Arts Collection now consists of more than 1,000 pieces of painted decorative art, the largest collection of exclusively painted works of decorative art in this country.

The DAC is proud to be celebrating its Silver Anniversary in 2007.

MISSION STATEMENT OF THE DAC

The mission of the Decorative Arts Collection is to promote understanding and appreciation of decorative painting by saving outstanding and significant historic and contemporary works, maintaining exhibitions and providing educational opportunities to the public.

This mission is the guiding force behind all decisions made by the board of trustees. The work of the DAC relies on annual financial contributions from individuals and corporations. Join the Friends of the DAC and help us continue the work begun over 25 years ago. Celebrate with us our heritage, and our future.

painting like
THE MASTERS

ONE OF THE ENDURING QUALITIES of decorative painting is how graciously and generously the artform is passed down from teacher to student, from friend to friend and from master to beginner. On the following pages are comprehensive step-by-step painting demonstrations contributed by 15 of the most beloved masters in the field of decorative arts. These projects are offered in celebration of the 25th Anniversary of the Decorative Arts Collection and include many of the styles and traditions that have been passed down through the years. Jo Sonja Jansen offers an exuberant polychrome teapot in traditional folk art style, while Peggy Harris paints baby deer with quiet colors and gentle humor. Gretchen Cagle's richly colored plums contrast with Ginger Edwards' sweet violas, while Andy Jones' birds and berries capture the historic precedence of Peter Ompir. The projects on the following pages are yours to enjoy and learn from, with grateful thanks to all those who have led the way.

planting creative seeds

HELEN BARRICK, MDA

WHEN WE TEACH we are planting creative seeds in our students' minds, giving them the means of applying that knowledge and hopefully creating the desire and inspiring the challenge to go further. Imagination is the fertilizer sprinkled on the creative seeds, opening the doors and revealing results we've only dreamed of. The DAC started as a creative seed of an idea and with time, effort and imagination has revealed results we could only dream of!

MATERIALS

BRUSHES
Loew-Cornell:
- 10/0 Liner series 7350
- no. 1 JS Liner
- nos. 1, 3, 4 Round series 7040
- no. 6 Filbert series 7500
- no. 6, 8, 10, 12, 14 Shader series 7300
- 3⁄4-inch (19mm) Wash/Glaze series 7150

Royal Aqualon Wisp:
- 1⁄4-inch (6mm), 1/8-inch (3mm) series 2935

JO SONJA ARTIST'S GOUACHE PALETTE
Warm White, Smoked Pearl, Skin Tone Base, Naples Yellow Hue, Turners Yellow, Gold Oxide, Raw Sienna, Burnt Sienna, Cadmium Orange, Red Earth, Brown Madder, Sapphire, Moss Green, Oakmoss, Olive Green, Teal Green, Nimbus Grey, Fawn, Brown Earth, Raw Umber

ADDITIONAL MATERIALS
- Jo Sonja Clear Glazing Medium, Retarder Medium, Kleister Medium
- Polyurethane Satin Varnish
- Gray graphite paper
- Medium-grit sandpaper
- Paper towel
- Stylus
- Masking tape
- Plastic container with lid for paint

SURFACE
Wooden tray by Country Pleasures
www.crewscountrypleasures.com,
417-759-7839

These patterns may be hand-traced or
photocopied. Enlarge the main pattern at
189% and the flower border pattern enlarge
at 200%, then enlarge at 114% to bring them
up to full size.

BACKGROUND

Sky: Palette-blend a little Smoked Pearl into the left side of a 3/4-inch (19mm) wash brush. Starting in the center, add larger clouds using "C" strokes and fading colors on the sides. Softly fade out bottom of clouds. Highlight some clouds with a little side load of Warm White. Add birds (curved lines) with 10/0 liner and thinned Raw Umber.

Distant trees: Retarder-dampen tree area and lightly into sky area. Blot lightly. Dampen a no. 10 flat brush with Retarder; blot brush and side load a little Teal Green and Brown Earth. Lightly dab in soft touches of color at the bottom of the trees, fading slightly upwards. Blot brush and with Moss Green + Naples Yellow Hue, dab in lighter foliage, fading color up into sky.

House: Lightly paint sides with Nimbus Grey. Shade a little with medium gray, Sapphire + Raw Umber + Nimbus Grey. Highlight front of house with Smoked Pearl. Add Raw Umber windows. Add chimney with thinned Red Earth. Shade chimney with Brown Madder linework. Add chimney smoke with Smoked Pearl.

Barn: Paint sides with thinned Red Earth. Shade with Brown Madder. Add roof with medium gray, Sapphire + Raw Umber + Nimbus Grey. Add weather-vane with thinned Raw Umber.

Grassy area: With no. 8 flat brush, suggest a little path with thinned Raw Umber, letting color fade out as it comes forward. Starting at base of trees with Moss Green + Naples Yellow Hue and working forward, begin picking up a little more Moss Green. Lightly add some touches of thinned Olive Green here and there. Add clumps of grass with 1/8-inch (3mm) and 1/4-inch (6mm) wisp brush using thinned Olive Green and then some thinned Moss Green. A liner brush may also be used for adding additional grasses.

Garden area: Lightly brush in touches of Fawn letting color fade out near the bottom area. Add thin Raw Umber shading for shadows and some Brown Earth. Highlight some areas with Fawn + Naples Yellow Hue.

1. DAISY TRIM

Pick up Kleister Medium with paint for texture and transparency in leaves and daisies. With no. 3 round, add leaves with transparent Olive Green. Add vines and veins on leaves with thin Olive Green linework.

Yellow Daisies: Pick up Kleister with each color as it is used. Undercoat daisy petal with no. 3 round and Raw Sienna. When dry, overstroke petals with Turners Yellow, leaving some Raw Sienna showing near the center. Add fine "gather lines" on the petals with thinned Burnt Sienna. Paint the center with thinned Red Earth. Add center dot and lower dots of Brown Madder. Upper dots are Cadmium Orange.

White Daisies: Pick up Kleister with each color as it is used. Undercoat the petals with Smoked Pearl + Oakmoss 1:1. When dry, overstroke petals with Warm White leaving some of the undercoat showing near the center. Add fine "gather lines" with thinned Raw Sienna + Raw Umber. Paint centers with thinned Gold Oxide. Add center dot and lower dots with Burnt Sienna. Upper dots are Turners Yellow.

2. PAINT AND SHADE CHILDREN

Paint in the children's faces, hair, arms and feet. Trace the hands and feet as accurately as possible. With thinned Skin Tone Base and a fine liner brush, go over the outer shapes of the face, arms and feet. Then with a no. 8 flat, basecoat all flesh areas with two smooth coats using Skin Tone Base. It is important to use shape-following strokes when basecoating the hair and flesh areas. Note: if needed, slightly thin the paint for smoother base- coating. Keep the outer edges of the hair wispy. Let dry. Trace the facial features, finger separations and hairlines on carefully with gray graphite. Go over these lines with a liner brush and thinned Burnt Sienna. When dry, erase any graphite lines.

For shading, mix dark flesh, 3 parts Burnt Sienna + 1 part Skin Tone Base. Place mixture on palette. Retarder

dampen face and remove excess with no. 14 brush. With a no. 3 round, apply the dark flesh mixture next to the hairline and into the neck. Blot and flatten the round brush tip and blend the shading into adjoining areas with a soft pat-pat stroke. Change to a dry no. 6 filbert to further soften the color. Note: shade between eye and eyebrow, then under nose and lower lip. Shade arms, knee and feet. Blending on faces, arms and feet should be smooth. Repeat shading where needed.

3. ADD BLUSH

Retarder dampen flesh areas and remove excess. Brush tiny amounts of Red Earth into tip of no. 3 round brush. Stroke on palette to remove some of the paint. Apply a little to side of cheek, blot brush and soften color across the cheek with pat-pat strokes. Further soften color with a pat-pat stroke of a dry no. 6 filbert brush, first the outer area of the cheek, then within the cheek color. With a flat-tened no. 1 round, add a little Red Earth to the center of the lower lip. Blot brush and lightly blend color toward the sides of the lip, letting color fade out. Shape the upper lip, letting color also fade out toward sides of the lip. Add a soft touch of Red Earth to the bottom of nose and chin. Add a touch of the blush color on arms, knee and feet, in plump areas next to shading. With Burnt Sienna and fine linework, add the nostrils and center

mouth line. Add finger separation lines. If needed, add fine linework to define the edges of the arms and feet.

4. EYES, HAIR AND FACIAL HIGHLIGHTS

Retarder dampen faces and remove excess. Palette blend a tiny amount of Warm White onto the corner of a no. 6 flat brush. Add highlights on the cheeks, nose and chin. With a fine liner brush add a little streak through the center of child's lower lip.

Fill in eyeballs with Burnt Sienna. Add a tiny Warm White dot for the highlight. Add the upper eyeline with a fine line of Burnt Sienna. Do not add a line on the bottom of the eye. Very lightly go over the eyebrow with thinned Burnt Sienna.

The hair has been basecoated with Skin Tone Base using shape-following strokes. A little linework is added to define the stroke direction. Let dry. With a no. 14 flat, brush a little Retarder over hair and remove excess before proceeding. With a flattened no. 4 round, tint hair with a transparent wash of color (see colors below) and let dry. Then, remoisten the hair with Retarder and add shading. For shading and adding highlights, use the 1/8-inch (3mm) and 1/4-inch (6mm) wisp brush and a 10/0 liner brush. Let dry. Remoisten hair with Retarder and add highlights. The wisp brush works beautifully when painting hair if you follow these suggestions: thin paint slightly with a little water and load paint into the tip of the brush. Use just the tip of the brush and very little pressure when applying the strokes. Reload the paint every two or three strokes. Test the loaded brush on the palette before applying.

Left child – tint hair with transparent Raw Sienna + a touch of Raw Umber. Shade with a little Raw Umber + Raw Sienna. Highlight with Naples Yellow Hue.

Right child – tint hair with transparent Gold Oxide. Shade with a little Burnt Sienna. Highlight with a tiny bit of Naples Yellow Hue + Gold Oxide.

5. CLOTHING

Basecoat clothing with one coat. Let dry. Trace pattern lines on. Apply Retarder over articles of clothing. Blot brush and remove excess Retarder. With sideloaded no. 10 or 12 brush, apply shading. Blot brush and blend with dabby strokes. Let dry.

6. CLOTHING DETAILS

Highlight clothing: Then add details using the liner brush and shade color. Let dry. Add tinting with transparent color.

Child on left: Basecoat shirt with mixture of Naples Yellow Hue and Red Earth 2:1. Shade with Brown Madder + Gold Oxide. Highlight with Naples Yellow Hue + Turners Yellow and Red Earth. Add Brown Madder stitching on sleeve hem and touches in creases where needed.

Pants and suspenders: Base with Medium Gray, Sapphire + Raw Umber + Nimbus Grey. Shade with dark gray, Sapphire + Raw Umber. Highlight with Nimbus Grey. Paint knee patches with Sapphire + Nimbus Grey. Add Turners Yellow cross checks and Nimbus Grey stitching. The button is Nimbus Grey outlined with dark gray. Use dark gray mix for stitching and line work.

Seed bag: Base with Fawn. Shade with Brown Earth. Highlight with Naples Yellow Hue + Fawn, then with more Naples Yellow Hue. Add Brown Earth drawstring. The seeds are Raw Umber and then some Naples Yellow Hue.

Child on right: Base shirt with Light Gray, Nimbus Gray and Smoked Pearl 1:1. Shade with Medium Gray, Nimbus Grey + a tiny bit of Sapphire and Raw

Umber. Highlight with Warm White. Let dry. Add check lines with thinned Turners Yellow and a little Gold Oxide. In shadow areas darken lines with a little Gold Oxide linework. Using shade color add fine linework where needed—to define and edge here and there, creases, etc.

Overalls: Base with medium blue mix, Sapphire + Nimbus Grey. Shade with darker blue, Sapphire + a little Raw Umber. Highlight with a light blue of Smoked Pearl + a little Sapphire, then further highlight with more Smoked Pearl. Add buttons on straps with a darker blue of Sapphire + Raw Umber. With darker blue linework add stitching and clean up linework where needed.

Straw hat: Base with Fawn. Shade with Brown Earth + Burnt Sienna.

Add rows of short strokes for straw. Using short strokes add highlights of Naples Yellow Hue + a little Raw Sienna, then further highlight with Naples Yellow Hue.

Garden hoe: Base the blade with a dark gray of Nimbus Grey + a little Sapphire + Raw Umber. Shade along the upper right and lower left areas with Sapphire + Raw Umber. Highlight along the upper side with Smoked Pearl + a little Nimbus Grey. Base the handle with Fawn. Shade along the lower side with Raw Umber + Brown Earth. Highlight along the upper side with Raw Sienna + Naples Yellow Hue. Add dirt with smudges on hoe with Raw Umber and a little Brown Earth.

Dirt smudges on clothing and feet: Brush Retarder over dried area, removing excess. With a no. 8 flat brush, palette-blend a little Raw Umber and Brown Earth in the brush, blot lightly on paper towel and add a few soft smudges of color on pants, feet, etc. Pile a little dirt in front of feet with Raw Umber and Brown Earth.

Tinting: Enhances and further develops the medium and dark areas of the clothing, background and children's neck areas. When painting is completely dry, brush a light coating of Retarder over a figure or area. Remove excess. With transparent color such as Burnt Sienna or Teal Green add transparent tints in areas needing a bit more dark value or color interest. Let dry. Small touches of Cadmium Orange may be added in a few places, medium dark areas in some clothing, barn, etc.

Long grass: With a no. 1 liner brush and very thin paint, add lots of various lengths of grasses at bottom of tray using Olive Green + a little Raw Umber, then add some very thin Raw Umber grasses.

hydrangea cottage

TRUDY BEARD, CDA

I LOVE THE FACT that a permanent collection of decorative art has been preserved for all to enjoy. It is important to recognize the rich heritage of decorative painting and to continue to add to our collection with works representing past and current artists. Ours is a unique art form that can be achieved by many and enjoyed by everyone.

This painting is my dream cottage, in a lovely field near the ocean, surrounded by a charming picket fence and blue hydrangeas and lots of birds.

MATERIALS

BRUSHES
Royal & Langnickel:
- 10/0 Royal Majestic Series 4585 Liner
- nos. 2, 4, 6, 8, 12 Royal Majestic Series 4150 Flats

FOLKART ACRYLIC COLORS
Dove Grey, Magenta, Violet Pansy

FOLKART ARTISTS' PIGMENTS
Aqua, Burnt Carmine, Burnt Umber, Cobalt, Dioxazine Purple, Hauser Green Dark, Hauser Green Light, Raw Sienna, Turner's Yellow, Warm White

ADDITIONAL MATERIALS
2-inch (51mm) sponge brush
Water-base wood sealer
Sandpaper
Paper towels
Light gray transfer paper
Tracing paper
Fine-tip stylus
FolkArt Blending Gel Medium

SURFACE
10-1/2 x 17-inch (26.7 x 43.2 cm) wooden frame with insert. Available from: Trudy Beard Designs 121 Calvin Park Blvd. Rockford, IL 61107 www.trudybearddesigns.com

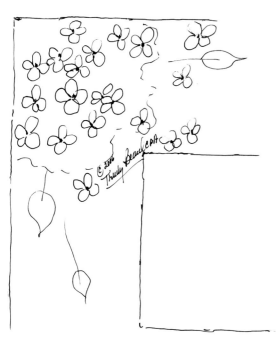

These patterns may be hand-traced or photocopied. Enlarge the main pattern at 147% and the hydrangea frame patterns enlarge at 200%, then enlarge at 114% to bring them up to full size.

1. HYDRANGEAS ON FRAME

Load a no.12 flat with Blending Gel; blot. Load same brush with Dioxazine Purple + Burnt Carmine; stroke in dark values. Pick up Cobalt; stroke in more dark values. Add a few strokes of Aqua.

Add some mid values with Cobalt + a bit of Dove Grey. Note: the outer edges of the blossoms are very loosely painted at this point.

2. MIDDLE AND LIGHT VALUES ON HYDRANGEAS

Use nos. 12 and 8 flats to stroke in middle and light values with the following colors: Dove Grey + Cobalt; Dove Grey + Aqua; Dove Grey + Violet Pansy; Dove Grey + Cobalt + Aqua; any color mixes above + a bit of Warm White; color mix above + a bit of Hauser Green Light.

3. DETAILING THE HYDRANGEAS

Use a 10/0 liner to loosely outline a few of the individual blossoms with the lighter color mixes, thinned with water.

Load Dioxazine Purple onto the liner and dot in the centers. Highlight the centers with small dabs of Turner's Yellow.

Load a no.12 or 8 flat with Blending Gel; blot. Load the same brush with Dove Grey + Cobalt + a bit of Hauser Green Dark; stroke in the darkest leaves.

Using the same brush, load with Dove Grey + Hauser Green Light and stroke in the lightest leaves. Add more Blending Gel to the mixture for more subtle leaf shapes.

Use a 10/0 liner and light green values, thinned with water, to paint tendrils and to loosely outline some of the leaves.

4. LANDSCAPE

To create the sky, load a no.12 flat with Blending Gel; blot. Load the same brush with Dove Grey + Cobalt. Apply color using short, overlapping strokes of the brush. Pick up additional Dove Grey to paint a few cloud formations. Highlight the cloud shapes by applying a bit more Dove Grey.

Load the same "dirty" brush with the sky mix + a bit more Cobalt + a small amount of Hauser Green Light. Tap in distant trees with the corner tip of the brush. Note that the trees are irregularly shaped at the top.

Pick up more Dove Grey + Hauser Green Light on the same brush. Paint the distant field, beneath the trees, with smooth horizontal strokes of the brush. Highlight distant trees by dry-brushing with a bit of this lighter value green.

Load a no.12 flat with Blending Gel; blot. Load the same brush with Dove Grey + Cobalt + Hauser Green Light. Paint the field around the house, using smooth horizontal strokes. Pick up a bit of Hauser Green Dark on the dirty brush; paint shadows next to the right side of the cottage and in the foreground.

5. COTTAGE

Load a no. 8 flat with Burnt Umber + a small amount of Burnt Carmine and paint the roof.

Load a no. 2 flat with Blending Gel; blot. Load the same brush with Burnt Umber + Burnt Carmine; paint the windows and door. Note that the stroke is started at the top of the window or door and pulled straight down. Lift off the brush as you reach the bottom of the door or window.

Use the 10/0 liner and the same mix, thinned with water, to paint small flying birds (not the birds perched on the roof top). Paint small trees on each side of the cottage with the same brush and mix.

Load a no.2 flat with Burnt Carmine + Burnt Umber + a little Dove Grey; paint the dark side of chimney. Pick up a bit more Dove Grey and paint the light side of the chimney.

Load a no.12 or 8 flat with Warm White + Cobalt + a small amount of Hauser Green Dark; dab in bushes around the cottage using the corner tip of the brush.

6. DETAILING THE COTTAGE AND LANDSCAPE

Apply a color accent to the dark side of the cottage. Load a dry no. 8 flat with Dove Grey + Cobalt; blot. Lightly drybrush this mix on the shadow side of the cottage, starting at the top; pull downward.

Load a no. 8 flat with Hauser Green Light; blot. Drybrush over the roof to create the look of moss. Apply another coat if needed.

Apply a color accent of Dove Grey + Cobalt to the roof (apply a very small amount).

Highlight the roof with Warm White + a touch of Raw Sienna. Use a drybrush technique to apply highlight. Highlight the chimney with the same mix. Highlight the small tree trunks with Raw Sienna + Warm White on a 10/0 liner.

Use a 10/0 liner to outline the windows and add windowpanes with Warm White + Dove Grey, thinned with water. If you like, small lines in the windows will indicate tied-back curtains.

Load a no. 2 flat with Dove Grey + Cobalt and paint shutters and window boxes. Create slats on the shutters with tiny lines of Dove Grey.

Use a 10/0 liner and the following colors to dab in window box flowers and foliage: Magenta; Magenta + Warm White; Warm White; Raw Sienna + Burnt Carmine + a bit of Warm White (orange tones); Hauser Green Dark; Hauser Green Light.

To detail the grass and flowering bushes, load a no. 8 brush with the following various color mixes; dry-brush on the ground and the bushes to create color and texture: Aqua + a bit of Dove Grey; Aqua + a bit of Hauser Green Light; Cobalt + a bit of Dove Grey; Magenta + a bit of Dove Grey; Magenta + Warm White (pinks on tree); Violet Pansy + a bit of Warm White.

Load a 10/0 liner with a brush-mix of Burnt Umber + Cobalt, thin with water. Paint the perched birds on the rooftop.

To paint the fence, load a no. 8 flat with Blending Gel; blot. Load the same brush with Warm White; paint the larger fence boards. Paint the smaller boards with nos. 6 and 8 flats; use less paint as you paint the smaller fence boards in the shadowed area.

RONNIE BRINGLE

I FEEL SO BLESSED TO LIVE IN A FREE COUNTRY! I am so thankful for all the men and women who have given their time, their talents, and even their lives to keep our country free and to protect us from harm. This project is in honor of and dedicated to America's armed forces. God bless them—every one!

MATERIALS

BRUSHES
Bette Byrd:
- nos. 2, 4, and 6 Bringle Blenders
- no. 2 Flat Bringle Blender
- nos. 0, 00, 10/0 Liners series 400
- 3/4-inch (19mm) Flat series 250

JO SONJA ARTIST'S GOUACHE PALETTE
Brown Earth, Burnt Umber, Cadmium Yellow Mid, Colony Blue, Napthol Red Light, Payne's Grey, Raw Sienna, Red Earth, Sapphire, Smoked Pearl, Teal Green

COLOR MIXES
- *Blue Mix:* 4 parts Payne's Grey + 1 part Sapphire
- *Gold Mix #1:* Raw Sienna + just a touch of Red Earth
- *Gold Mix #2:* 6 parts Cadmium Yellow Mid + 1 part Red Earth
- *Red Mix #1:* 3 parts Napthol Red Light + 1 part Payne's Grey
- *Red Mix #2:* 1 part Napthol Red Light + 1 part Payne's Grey

ADDITIONAL MATERIALS
- Jo Sonja's All Purpose Sealer
- Jo Sonja's Polyurethane Gloss Varnish
- Jo Sonja's Polyurethane Matte Varnish
- Jo Sonja's Clear Glazing Medium
- 3-inch (7.6 cm) sponge trim roller
- Sea sponge
- Tracing paper
- Transfer paper

SURFACE
19-1/4 x 13-1/4 x 6-inch (48.9 x 33.7 x 15.2 cm) Tile Tray #T111 from: Unique Woods
2800 W. Division Street A1
Arlington, TX 76012
www.uniquewoods.com
phone 817-795-9650

This pattern may be hand-traced or photocopied. Enlarge at 200%, then enlarge at 125% to bring up to full size.

RED AND WHITE ELEMENTS

Step 1 photo: All red and white elements are painted the same way. To undercoat, use a no. 2 or 4 Bringle Blender to blend with Smoked Pearl and Payne's Grey, creating medium and dark values.

Step 2 photo: When dry, blend and drybrush with more Payne's Grey to darken. Blend and drybrush with more Smoked Pearl to lighten.

BLUE ELEMENTS

Step 1 photo: All blue elements are painted the same way. Use a no. 2 or 4

Bringle Blender to blend with Blue Mix and Payne's Grey, creating mostly dark values.

Step 2 photo: When dry, blend and drybrush with more Payne's Grey to darken.

Step 3 photo: Blend and drybrush with Sapphire and Sapphire + Colony Blue to highlight and tint. On the blue heart, paint the star with Smoked Pearl and drybrush lightly to shade with Payne's Grey. On the hat band, paint the stars with Gold Mix #2. Drybrush lightly to shade and tint with Red Mix

#1. Stipple just a little in the centers with Cadmium Yellow Mid. Paint the narrow trim line between the stripes and the blue band with Gold Mix #2. Tint with Red Mix #1, then with Brown Earth and highlight with Smoked Pearl. On the shield, paint the stars with Smoked Pearl and outline with Gold Mix #2. Paint the narrow trim line between the stripes and the blue band with Gold Mix #2. Tint with Red Mix #1. Shade with Brown Earth, and highlight with Smoked Pearl.

1. BASE THE ELEMENTS

To paint the red heart, use a no. 4 or 6 Bringle Blender to blend with Red Mix #1 and Red Mix #2. Let dry.

To paint the gold star, use a no. 2 Bringle Blender to blend with Gold Mix #2 and Red Mix #1. Repeat for better blending and add more Gold Mix #2 to lighten.

To paint the eagle, use a no. 2 flat Bringle Blender to whisk the feathers on the wings with Brown Earth, then whisk again with Burnt Umber and with Raw Sienna. Use the flat brush to whisk the head and neck with Smoked Pearl. Let dry.

To paint the leaves, stems and berries, use a no. 2 or 4 Bringle Blender to paint the leaves with mixes of any of the colors on your palette. Don't make them too bright green, but use a lot of red and brown with the greens and yellows. Paint the berries with Red Mix #1. Let dry, then stipple to highlight with Napthol Red Light. Drybrush to shade with Red Mix #2.

2. SHADE THE ELEMENTS

For the red heart, blend and drybrush with more Red Mix #2 to shade the heart.

To paint the white star, use a no. 2 Bringle Blender to blend with Smoked Pearl and Payne's Grey, creating medium and dark values. Let dry, then blend and drybrush with Smoked Pearl to lighten and with Payne's Grey to darken, creating medium and light values.

For the gold star, add more Red Mix #1 to tint if needed and shade.

For the eagle, use more Burnt Umber to darken under the upper edge. Whisk just a little Smoked Pearl here and there to lighten. Also use the flat brush to whisk the upper edge of the wings with Raw Sienna and with Brown Earth. Whisk again lightly with Burnt Umber and let dry. Whisk again with Smoked Pearl. Use a liner brush to define some of the feathers with Smoked Pearl.

For the leaves, stems and berries, mix Teal Green and Burnt Umber for a brownish green to paint the stems and veins and to paint a light outline on the leaves. You may have to repeat the highlight and shade steps on the berries for a good blend.

3. HIGHLIGHT THE ELEMENTS

For the red heart, drybrush and blend to highlight with more Red Mix #1 and with Napthol Red Light. Let the heart dry and trace the pattern for the banner. Paint the banner using a no. 2 Bringle Blender to blend with Gold Mix #2 and Red Mix #1. Let dry, then blend and drybrush to shade with Red Mix #2 and a little Brown Earth. Add just a tiny bit of Burnt Umber in the very darkest areas where the

banner curls around the heart. Paint the edge of the banner with Smoked Pearl and lightly drybrush to shade the ends with Payne's Grey. Paint the lettering with Smoked Pearl, at least two coats.

For the white star, paint the edge of the star with Payne's Grey, at least two coats. Paint the inner star with Red Mix #1, at least two coats.

For the gold star, paint the stripe on the edge of the star with Red Mix #1 and paint the inner star with Red Mix #1.

For the eagle, paint the red stripes with Red Mix #1 and let dry. Use a liner brush or small Bringle Blender to shade the stripes with Payne's Grey and to highlight with Napthol Red Light. Whisk a few feathers of Smoked Pearl to highlight the head. Whisk a few feathers down over the banner and the shield. Paint the beak with Raw Sienna. Highlight

with Gold Mix #2 and with Cadmium Yellow Mid. Shade with Brown Earth and with Burnt Umber. Paint the nostril with Burnt Umber. Paint the eye with Raw Sienna. Paint the lid line at the top of the eye with Burnt Umber and shade on each side of the eye, on the feathers, with Burnt Umber. Shade the eye with Brown Earth. Paint the pupil and outline the eye with Burnt Umber.

For the leaves, stems, and berries, paint the sparkle with Smoked Pearl. Let some of the berries around the outer edge stay rather dark with more shading and less sparkle. You want the berries to blend in and become part of the supporting structure. Add a light accent to the stems and veins with a mix of Cadmium Yellow Mid, Teal Green and Smoked Pearl, painting just a tiny line with a liner brush.

an abundance of plums

GRETCHEN CAGLE, CDA

FOUNDED IN 1982, TWENTY-FIVE YEARS AGO, the DAC is now celebrating its silver anniversary. . . how fast the years have passed! Fortunately, in those early years, the SDP saw the need to save the history of our art form for future generations. Even then, some of the decorative painters of that era were in failing health and several of our painting heroes had already passed away. What to do but form a new entity to house this infant collection of contemporary decorative art. From those precious few paintings the Collection has grown to include decorative art from around the world. . . from the famous, the not so famous and the infamous. I am truly proud to be a part of a collection that actually documents my personal growth as a decorative painter from those early, not so famous, years to the present.

MATERIALS

BRUSHES
Kala Kolinsky:
- nos. 4, 6, 8, and 10 series 5250, short bristle flats
- no. 1 series 5100 liner

WINSOR & NEWTON ARTISTS' OIL COLORS
Bright Red, Cadmium Lemon, Ivory Black, Payne's Grey, Permanent Alizarin Crimson, Purple Madder, Titanium White, Yellow Ochre

DECOART AMERICANA ACRYLIC PAINT
Deep Burgundy

ADDITIONAL MATERIALS
Liberty Matte Finish
White graphite paper

SURFACE
10 x 20-inch (25.4 x 50.8 cm) stretched canvas, custom framed upon completion

This pattern may be hand-traced or photocopied. Enlarge at 133% to bring up to full size. The "L" indicates light value plums; the "D" indicates dark value plums.

BACKGROUND PREPARATION

Paint the canvas with several applications of DecoArt Deep Burgundy acrylic. When dry, spray the canvas with Liberty Matte Finish (available from Artists Supply Co., 4508 Winchell, Mantua, OH 44255, 330-562-9220). Transfer the pattern with white graphite paper.

PAINTING ORDER:

- Light value plums
- Dark value plums
- Leaves
- Border defining the interior background area
- Background inside the border
- Background outside the border
- Allow painting to dry and then paint the branches, water drops and tendrils.

PALETTE FOR LIGHT VALUE PLUMS:

- *Dark Area:* Permanent Alizarin Crimson
- *Light Area:* Permanent Alizarin Crimson + a small amount of Bright Red
- *Shade:* Purple Madder
- *1st Highlight:* Payne's Grey + Titanium White
- *2nd Highlight:* Titanium White + Payne's Grey
- *Final Highlight:* Titanium White

PALETTE FOR DARK VALUE PLUMS:

- *Base:* Permanent Alizarin Crimson
- *Shade:* Purple Madder
- *1st Highlight:* Payne's Grey + Titanium White
- *2nd Highlight:* Titanium White + Payne's Grey

PALETTE FOR LEAVES:

- *Base:* Cadmium Lemon + Titanium White + a small amount of Ivory Black
- *Shade:* Base mixture + Ivory Black
- *Highlight:* Titanium White
- *Tint:* Yellow Ochre, Red and red-violet mixtures from the plums

1. BASE IN PLUMS AND LEAVES

Light Value Plums: Apply Light and Dark Value on each plum and blend. The light comes from the upper left of the design; therefore, the dark areas fall on the right side of each plum (opposite the light source). On a round object the dark value takes the shape of a crescent falling on the right side of the object just inside its outer edge. Additionally, apply dark value within the plunge area of each plum. Light Value will complete the block-in of color on the plum. Blend with short, choppy, irregular strokes creating the splotchy color variations within the plums.

Dark Value Plums: Place Dark and Light Value on each plum. These are not only darker in value but cooler in temperature thus causing them to recede. Keep colors a bit splotchy. Since most of these plums are tucked into the background of the cluster, they will have less detail and be duller, and have less defined highlights on them. Be sure to keep the overlaps between the light value and dark value plums dark and well-defined.

Leaves: Base with a mid-value green color allowing for value changes within the base color. Add a few splotches of Yellow Ochre, barely blending, then shade at the stem ends, down the center vein areas and inside the folds.

Branch: Remember, paint this when the background areas behind it are dry. Base and then apply shade randomly along the lower edge of the branch and in the forks between branches, barely blending the color with the base color.

2. STRENGTHEN SHADES AND HIGHLIGHTS

Plums: Strengthen the shaded crescent areas with a splotch of darker value applied in the 4-5 o'clock position and barely blend. Where two plums overlap and a triangular corner forms, shade these areas darker in value. Apply the 1st Highlight and blend it with choppy strokes, thus creating some of the mottled, naturally splotchy colors that appear on plums.

Leaves: Refine the blending process so that strokes follow the natural outward growth pattern from the center vein area toward the tip of the leaf. Strengthen highlights, again following the growth patterns.

Branch: Apply highlights randomly along the upper edge of the branch, barely blending the colors allowing them to remain a bit splotchy.

3. FINAL HIGHLIGHTS AND LEAF DETAILS

Plums: Allow the plums to dry, then continue to brighten by adding a second highlight made by adding more Titanium White to the previously used grey mix. Barely blend, keeping it splotchy for detail and interest. Apply the final highlight, barely blending it and perhaps leaving it just a bit more detailed with a splotchy glint. Strengthen shaded areas if necessary to create greater dimension between the plums.

Leaves: This step may be done either on a dry surface or while the previous step is still wet. Strengthen highlights if necessary. Add bug bites, applying them with the color of the object that would naturally appear behind the leaves. Add tints of plum colors along leaf edges and in shadow areas. Using the chisel edge of a flat brush loaded with the leaf base color, apply center veins just inside the dark/light separations and side veins radiating in the same direction as the previously determined growth pattern.

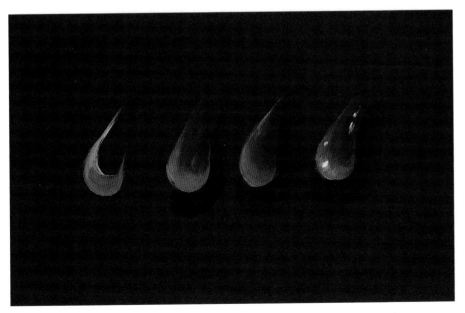

4. WATER DROPLETS

Using a no. 4 flat brush loaded with Titanium White, shape the drop with a U-stroke. Start on the chisel edge at the upper left, pull down, adding pressure to the brush to flatten it along the bottom of the drop. Let up on the pressure, pulling back to the chisel edge on the right side.

Dry-wipe the brush and blend into the background color. Apply a cast shadow with the dry-wiped brush using a value darker than the subject color.

Dry-wipe the brush and blend the cast shadow. Using Titanium White loaded onto the corner of the flat brush or a liner brush, apply highlight glints.

GINGER EDWARDS

I AM SO PLEASED TO BE ASKED TO CONTRIBUTE a painting for this special 25th anniversary celebration of the DAC. As a past president of the Society of Decorative Painters, I had the opportunity to serve on the board of the DAC and I know firsthand how important the work of this organization is. I firmly believe in the preservation of our very special form of art. I want to be sure that future generations have the chance to see the beauty and variety of decorative painting. I urge you all to join in and support the DAC. I want to wish the DAC a very happy 25th anniversary and many years of productive growth in the future.

MATERIALS

BRUSHES
Bette Byrd Aqua Sable:
- nos. 2 and 4 round, series 100
- nos. 2, 8, 10 and 12 flats, series 200
- 10/0 liner, series 500

FOLKART ACRYLIC COLORS
Titanium White, Vintage White, Baby Blue, Periwinkle, Lavender, Dioxazine Purple, Thunder Blue, Green Umber, Yellow Ochre, Lemonade, Lime Yellow, Burnt Umber

ADDITIONAL MATERIALS
- Variegated metal leaf flakes and adhesive
- Natural sea sponge
- Rustoleum aerosol automotive primer
- Fine grit sandpaper
- Tracing paper
- Gray transfer paper and stylus
- FolkArt Floating Medium
- Brush-on varnish

SURFACE
Jar candle with wooden or metal lid

This pattern may be hand-traced or photo-copied. Enlarge at 103% to bring it up to full size.

PREPARATION

1. Sand lid (whether wooden or metal) with fine-grit sandpaper to dull the surface. Wipe surface clean of sanded particles.
2. Spray lid with primer. Let dry completely.
3. Base paint lid with Baby Blue. Let dry completely.
4. Trace and transfer the design.
5. Measure and mark a 1⁄2-inch (13mm) border all around outside edge of lid. (A ceramist's/china painter's edging tool makes this easy.)
6. Sideload a no. 12 flat brush with small amounts of Periwinkle to float the out-side border. Rinse the brush and blend or tap with a damp sponge. Let dry, then spatter lightly with Periwinkle thinned to a very light value. Let dry.

PAINTING THE DESIGN

This design is quick and easy. The flower and leaves are established with flat brushes sideloaded with paint allowing the base paint to show within the design. Tints are floated using paint thinned with water + small amounts of Floating Medium to a transparent consistency. Highlights are drybrushed.

LETTERING

Thin Periwinkle with water to a semi-transparent consistency, then use the no. 2 flat brush to paint the letters. Let dry.

GOLD TRIM

To add the gold trim around the lid, dampen the sponge with water and squeeze dry, then lightly sponge metal leaf adhesive onto the edges of the lid. Do not apply adhesive too heavily. Let dry until the adhesive is clear, then apply metal leaf flakes. Allow the adhesive to completely dry, then buff with a soft cloth to remove excess. Brush on a pro-tective coating of your favorite varnish.

1. BASE IN PETALS AND LEAVES

Sideload a no. 10 or 12 flat with Peri-winkle and paint the top and middle petals. The lower petals are painted with Vintage White. Let dry.

Establish the leaves in two steps. Sideload a no. 10 or 12 flat with Green Umber and stroke color across the back (stem end) of each leaf and next to the center vein on one side of leaf. Let dry.

Sideload the same brush with Green Umber, position the brush so that the "paint side" touches the outside edge of the leaf and stroke paint onto the leaf. Let dry.

2. DETAIL PETALS AND LEAVES

Sideload a no. 8 or 10 flat with Dioxa-zine Purple + a touch of Thunder Blue to shade the petals. Stroke shading in the throat and along the edges of the top and middle petals first, then the bottom petal. Let dry.

Indicate a few veins in the top and

middle petals using a liner and the shading mixture thinned to an inky consistency. Let dry.

Sideload a flat brush with small amounts of Lavender thinned to a transparent consistency and tint the petals. Let dry.

Drybrush highlights using a no. 2 or 4 round brush loaded with Titanium White + a touch of Periwinkle for the top and middle petals. The lower petal is highlighted with Vintage White + a small amount of Titanium White.

With a 10/0 liner, indicate the pistil in the throat with Lemonade + a touch of Green Umber. Paint markings on the lower petal (next to the throat) with Yellow Ochre, highlight with Lemonade. Paint bold lines with Dioxazine Purple + a bit of Green Umber.

Use the tip of the liner to add pollen to each side petal. First tap on Yellow Ochre, then highlight with Lemonade.

Establish the viola stems with thinned Green Umber. Let dry, then shade the stem with a flat brush sideloaded with Green Umber + a touch of Thunder Blue or Burnt Umber. Let dry, then highlight the stem with Lime Yellow + a tiny bit of Titanium White.

Shade the leaves next to the center vein and outside edges using a no. 10 or 12 flat sideloaded with Green Umber + a tiny bit of Burnt Umber or Thunder Blue. Let dry.

Load a no. 2 or 4 round brush with small amounts of Lime Yellow + tiny amounts of Titanium White and drybrush highlights on the leaves.

Paint veins in leaves using a 10/0 liner. The center vein is Lime Yellow + tiny bit of Titanium White. The side veins are the same mixture on the dark areas of each leaf; on the light areas use Green Umber + a touch of Thunder Blue or Burnt Umber.

painter's delight

HEIDI ENGLAND

T HOUGHTS ON A SILVER ANNIVERSARY: It's a painter's delight! As we celebrate 25 years, I can't help but remember the three artists whose works are the foundation of decorative painting and the Decorative Arts Collection—Peter Hunt, Peter Ompir, and Per Lysne. Aspects of their work continue to influence and inspire my painting as I create new works today. And yes, silver is the promise of gold—a golden anniversary to come!

MATERIALS

BRUSHES
Jo Sonja's Sure Touch:
- 3/8-inch (10mm), 1/4-inch (6mm) and 1-inch (25mm) oval glaze, series 1390
- nos. 2 and 6 filbert, series 1385
- no. 1 detailer, series 1355

JO SONJA'S CHROMA ACRYLICS
Poppy, Tiger Lily, Marigold, Mustard Seed, Primrose, Vellum, Vines, Raindrop, Cornflower, Harbour Blue, Wild Grape, Blackberry, Island Sand, Linen, Burnt Umber, Silver, Pale Gold, Rich Gold

ADDITIONAL MATERIALS
- Chroma's Clear Glazing Medium, Retarder, and Polyurethane Water-Based Gloss Varnish
- Clapham's Beeswax Salad Bowl Finish
- White gesso
- Texture paste

SURFACE
16-inch (40.6cm) round, triple beaded wooden bowl, available from:
Paul Loftness
3244 651st Ave.
Gibbon, MN 55335
Phone: 507-834-6948

This pattern may be hand-traced or photocopied. Enlarge at 200%, then enlarge at 102% to bring up to full size.

BASIC PREPARATION
Seal the surface with one part White Gesso, to one part Texture Paste. Dry. Paint the middle inside area with Raindrop with a touch of Linen. Paint the lettering area Linen. Overstroke with Silver. The outer area is Rich Gold. Overstroke with Pale Gold. The three beads are painted as follows: Tiger Lily for the bead closest to the center, Cornflower for the middle bead, and Poppy for the outer bead. The ledge by the Cornflower bead is Raindrop. Overstroke with Island Sand dots and Blackberry dots. Paint and drybrush all indented areas with Blackberry. Dry well.

1. BACKGROUND

With a 3/8-inch (10mm) oval glaze brush, paint the mountains a mixture of Wild Grape and Blackberry. Use Marigold with a touch of Island Sand for the middle ground and Mustard Seed with a touch of Primrose for the foreground. Use Wild Grape to create the small mound under the painter's feet. Add dabs of Blackberry for the impression of trees and shrubs at the base of the mountains, the base of the orange and yellow areas and at the Wild Grape mound. Brush mix Vines, Harbour Blue, and a touch of Blackberry and use the same oval glaze brush to stipple the outer greenery. Dry all well. Erase graphite lines.

2. PAINTING LADY

Use the no. 2 filbert to brush-mix one part Marigold to one part Island Sand and create a middle-value flesh color. Begin with the hands, then the neck, and lastly the face. Let the color begin to dry and then add Tiger Lily and a touch of Poppy for a peasant cheek.

Mix Mustard Seed with a touch of Blackberry for a soft autumn brown. Use this color for the huge palette and the paintbrush bristles. Add a touch of Island Sand to the brown mix and drybrush a highlight onto the middle of the palette.

Use a 1/4-inch (6mm) oval glaze brush and Harbour Blue to paint the lady's right arm. The body of the dress is Cornflower, and the left arm is Cornflower plus a touch of Raindrop. Use the no. 2 filbert and Blackberry to paint the shoes, hair, and the brush handle. Dry well. Erase graphite lines.

3. PAINTING LADY DETAILS

Use a no. 6 filbert and Blackberry for the dress's dark vertical stripes and mix Mustard Seed and Primrose for the yellow stripes. Add more Poppy to her cheek and use the no. 2 filbert to add Poppy dots to the dress. Paint the hem with Island Sand. Use the no. 1 detailer for the Poppy red hair ribbon. Her features are Blackberry. Her mouth is Poppy with Island Sand highlights.

Drybrush Blackberry on the palette to shade. Add a touch of red, yellow, orange, green, blue, and grape to the palette. Highlight the paint spots on the palette and the detail on the left sleeve with the Linen and Island Sand mix.

Use a no. 2 filbert to highlight the brush bristles with the Island Sand and Tiger Lily mix. Shade by drybrushing with Blackberry. Use Linen to drybrush a metal ferrule onto the brush handle. Highlight with touches of Island Sand.

4. LETTERING

Use Blackberry on a no. 2 filbert for all the letters and numbers. Form them using a combination of lines, commas, tears, S-strokes and C-strokes. Follow your pattern lines for each letter. This will help you with the slant of the letters and the spacing. There are small spaces between the components of the letters to show the strokes used.

There is a little extra space to each side of the years. Add hearts. Paint these hearts with the no. 2 filbert. Paint two commas that meet toward the lower edge. One side is Poppy, the other is Tiger Lily. Shade under the hearts with a touch of Blackberry.

5. FLORAL BORDER—STEP 1

Use a 3/8-inch (10mm) oval glaze brush to drybrush Blackberry leaves around the flowers. These appear to be shadows and give depth. Stroke toward the stem line. Then paint the leaves using Vines with a touch of Harbour Blue. Begin with the larger leaves around the three large roses and go smaller as you extend outward.

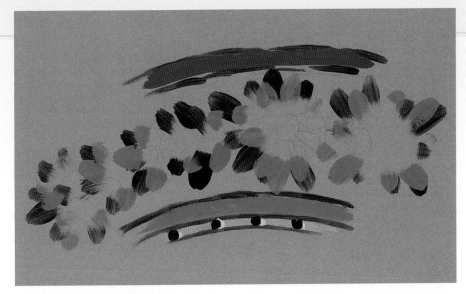

6. FLORAL BORDER—STEP 2

Use a no. 6 filbert to paint the roses with Poppy plus a very small touch of Tiger Lily. The heart of the roses and shaded area is drybrushed with Blackberry. The loose overstrokes are Poppy plus touches of Marigold and Mustard Seed.

Paint the Edelweiss petals with Linen + a touch of Vellum on a no. 6 filbert. Dab Vines with a touch of Vellum onto the centers. The blue flower, Enzian, is based with Cornflower. The center heart is Blackberry. Let some of the gold background show.

7. FLORAL BORDER—STEP 3

Add Harbour Blue to the shaded side of the Enzian and a touch of Cornflower and Raindrop for the highlight. The lower front petal is Raindrop. The side and back petals are Cornflower. The center dot of the Enzian is the Mustard Seed and Primrose mixture. The calyx is the Vines and Harbour Blue mix. Dry well. Erase pattern lines.

Use a no. 2 filbert and Primrose with a touch of Vellum to paint the center seeds on the Edelweiss. Add touches of blue Cornflower near the lower edge of the center. Re-stroke a few of the petals with Linen plus Island Sand. Add a few textured dabs of Poppy near the lower part of the roses and rosebuds. Add a few lines of Cornflower for blue accents near the lower part of the rose bowl and rose centers. The seed dots for all roses and buds are the Primrose and Mustard Seed mixture. Overstroke some leaves with the Vines and Harbour Blue mix plus a touch of Vellum for a lighter green.

white christmas

PEGGY HARRIS

HAPPY BIRTHDAY, DAC! The Decorative Arts Collection is truly a testament to the endurance of the creative spirit across time and place and serves to remind each of us of the fabulous and enduring tradition we all particpate in when we beautify an everyday object with our painting.

For me, the particular enticement of the decorative arts is the challenge of designing for the three-dimensional surface. In "White Christmas" I invite the eye to not only view the painting, but to explore the octagonal surface—leading the eye to walk around the box with the fawns until the surface and the painting become one piece of art, neither complete without the other. "White Christmas" tells the story of tiny woodland creatures sharing the spirit of the season on this snowy Christmas morning.

MATERIALS

BRUSHES
Peggy Harris Ultra Fur Set Series PH-250S by Silver Brush, Limited:
- nos. 1 and 2 Grand Prix Series 1000S white bristle rounds
- 1/8-inch (3mm) Ruby Satin Series 2528S filbert grass comb
- no. 2 Ruby Satin Series 2502S bright
- 20/0 Ultra Mini Series 2407S script liner
- 12/0 Ultra Mini Series 2406S angular
- 1/8-inch (3mm) & 1/4-inch (6mm) Wee Mops
- Peggy's Ultimate Varnish Brush

Brushes available through www.peggyharris.com

FOLKART ARTISTS' PIGMENT COLORS:
Asphaltum, Burnt Sienna, Burnt Umber, Fawn, Hauser Green Light, Medium Yellow, Pure Black, Red Light, Sap Green, Titanium White, True Burgundy

FOLKART ACRYLIC COLORS:
- *Gold mix:* Metallic Sahara Gold + touch Metallic Christmas Green
- *Silver mix:* Metallic Sterling Silver + Metallic Pearl White 1:1

ADDITIONAL MATERIALS
- FolkArt Blending Gel Medium
- FolkArt Clear Cote Matte Acrylic Spray
- Tracing paper
- Mechanical pencil
- Stylus
- Gray transfer paper
- Kneaded eraser
- Masterson Art Products Sta-Wet Handy Palette
- Brush basin
- Soft paper towels
- Q-tips Cotton Swabs
- Hair (or embossing) dryer
- Magnifying glass (Magnabrite)
- Fine-grit sandpaper
- #400 grit wet/dry sandpaper
- Tack cloth
- J. W., etc. First Step Wood Sealer
- J. W., etc. Under Cover (gesso)
- J. W., etc. Right Step Satin Varnish
- J. W., etc. Painter's Finishing Wax
- #0000 white synthetic steel wool pad
- Surface
- Octagonal wood box of choice

TIPS BEFORE STARTING

- This is a wet-in-wet technique, so choose paints and gel that have the greatest open time, and always use a wet palette.

- Keep acrylic gel in a small separate container, as it tends to "melt" into a wet palette.

- Always paint gel over fur areas, and areas to be blended, before applying paint.

- Paint and complete small areas at a time (like a hip or a forehead), establishing the highlights before the paint dries. (Shading may be painted over dry paint later.)

- Dry the paint with a hair dryer before adding successive layers of gel and paint to prevent surprise lifting of paint that appears dry.

- Once color has been applied, manipulate the gel and the paint with clean brushes. Frequently wipe clean and re-moisten your brushes with gel as you work.

- Use a "feather touch." The bristles and hairs of your brushes should never bend as you manipulate the paint over the surface.

- Use a clean, wet, bright brush as an "eraser" to sharpen shapes or lift out mistakes.

- Repeat the gel and paint layers infinite times to brighten highlights, deepen shading, add color glazes, or simply add more fluff. Keep layering until you've achieved the desired look.

- Experiment with different proportions of gel-to-paint to create delicate effects and promote blending.

This pattern may be hand-traced or photocopied. Enlarge at 108% to bring it up to full size.

PREPARATION

Sand the box. Wipe clean with a tack cloth. Seal the box. Dry. For a super smooth surface, gesso the top. Dry and re-sand. Remove dust with a tack cloth.

Base paint the box. Paint the outside of the box base with Titanium White; the base bottom and inside with metallic gold mix. Paint the top of the lid with Titanium White; the bands with metallic gold mix and the silver mix. Paint the underside of the lid with the silver mix and the outer rim with the gold mix. Dry.

Spray the base-painted box generously with matte acrylic spray. Dry well.

Carefully trace and transfer the design with gray transfer paper. (These are very tiny animals. Even the smallest deviation in tracing and transferring may result in a misshapen animal.)

Lighten transfer lines with a kneaded eraser until barely visible so they will not show under fur edges.

TECHNIQUES

Because this is a very small, delicate design, use much less gel and paint than is usual in my method. Remember: less is best. Build transparent layers gradually. Often it will be easier to "correct" your painting than to paint so accurately in the first place. Use the clean, wet bright brush as an eraser to sharpen shapes or lift out mistakes. Check your painting under the magnifying glass every now and then. Rely heavily on the 20/0 liner to create tiny details.

1. SNOWY BACKGROUND
Please refer to the photo of the finished project on page 52 to see the background. Spread a scant amount of gel over gray shadow areas. Quickly paint the area with brush-mixed dark gray (Pure Black + Titanium White).

Immediately blend the gray into the white background with a dry mop. Wipe the mop clean frequently as you work for even blending into the white areas.

While still wet, lift out the snowy tree branches with a wet Q-tip or a wet bright brush. If needed, blend with a tiny mop. Dry and repeat for deeper shading if needed.

In the same manner, create hoof hollows and shadows around the birds and animals. Let dry.

2. FAWNS, CHIPMUNKS AND BIRDLETS
Starting with the fawns, use the large end of a stylus dipped in Pure Black to mark each eye placement. They will be

perfected later. Paint the noses Pure Black with a 20/0 liner.

Paint the inside of the ears with brush-mixed pink (Titanium White + Red Light). Dry.

Apply a thin layer of gel to the ears and head of a fawn. Pick up a tiny amount of Fawn with the bristle brush and stroke in rows of extremely short fur. While the paint is still wet, lift out any highlights and stray paint in white fur areas with a wet Q-tip or bright brush. Blend highlight areas into the surrounding fur with a clean bristle brush. Wipe the brush clean frequently as you blend and continue to groom the fur. More gel and/ or paint may be added as you work.

Gel, paint, and highlight the remainder of the fawn, one area at a time. Dry with a hairdryer until no moisture glistens in the light.

Paint the chipmunk eyes with Pure Black and the tiny end of a stylus. Mark the ears with Burnt Umber and a 20/0 liner. Dry.

Apply a slick of gel to the chipmunks. Remove excess by touching with a finger. Stroke in extremely short fur with Fawn and the no. 1 bristle round. Remove highlighted areas with a wet bright brush, if needed, and blend back into surrounding fur with the bristle brush. Dry.

For the birdlets, paint each eye with the small end of a stylus and Pure Black. With the 20/0 liner and Burnt Umber, stroke in tiny beaks, wings, tails and head feathers. Dry with the hair dryer.

3. FAWNS, CHIPMUNKS AND BIRDLETS

Using the same blending and highlighting techniques as described in step 2, begin to strengthen the fawn's color. Apply gel to an area and blend in more Fawn where needed. (Since the gel dries invisible, I spread it over the entire animal, but only add touches of new paint here and there. The gel also enables me to see the true color of the fawn as it will appear after varnishing.) Dry with a hair dryer.

Re-gel the fawn. Using the 1/8-inch (3mm) grass comb, continue to make color adjustments and shade with Fawn and Burnt Umber. It is safest to always place some Fawn under Burnt Umber areas to prevent the fawn from looking dirty. Also, use more Fawn to blend Burnt Umber into surrounding fur. Repeat as needed. Use the 20/0 liner or

12/0 angular brushes to perfect the fur in small places. Dry with a hair dryer.

For the chipmunks, re-apply the gel slick and blend in Burnt Umber shading. Dry. Adjust the color using a 1/8-inch (3mm) grass comb and Burnt Sienna or Asphaltum + gel. Dry.

For the birdlets, apply a thin layer of gel to a birdlet and stroke in Fawn breast feathers with a 20/0 liner. Dry.

4. FAWNS, CHIPMUNKS AND BIRDLETS

Going back to the fawns, stroke in white ear fur with Titanium White and a 20/0 liner. Add more Fawn and Burnt Umber shading if needed. Paint tiny spots on the fawn's back with Titanium White.

Perfect the eye and nose with a 20/0 liner. Paint delicate lids and eyelashes with inky Pure Black. Add sparkling highlights of Titanium White to the eye and nose. Tint the muzzle with transparent pink.

For the chipmunks, use a 20/0 liner to paint the stripes with inky Pure Black and extend the tail fur with Burnt Umber.

For the birdlets, re-apply gel and adjust the colors using Fawn, Burnt Sienna, Burnt Umber, and the 12/0 angular or 20/0 liner. Repeat if needed. Perfect with a wet bright brush used as an eraser. Add

miniscule accents of Pure Black and Titanium White with a 20/0 liner.

5. HOLLY SPRIGS

Using tiny brushes, freehand the holly sprigs with Hauser Green Light. Shade with Sap Green + Pure Black. Clean up stems and leaf points with a wet bright brush. Accent with inky Pure Black.

Make tiny berries with Red Light and the end of a stylus. Connect the berries to the stems with a 20/0 liner and very inky green.

6. EMBELLISHMENTS

Freehand metallic gold mix garlands around the silver rim. Accent with a fluttering bow at each corner. Use a 20/0 liner heavily loaded with paint. Repeat the garland motif around the gold mix rim with the silver mix color.

7. FINISHING

Spatter the scene with snow using thinned Titanium White and a bristle brush flipped across a knife. Remove stray flakes from animals with a wet Q-tip. Add a few random flakes with the tip of a stylus.

Varnish the box with multiple coats of satin varnish. Do not sand between the early coats of varnish as you may abrade the delicate fur lines and color glazes.

For a lacquered look, apply over 20 coats of varnish, sanding between every few coats with wet-dry sandpaper.

Apply painter's finishing wax with a #0000 synthetic steel wool pad to enhance the varnish and bring out the beauty of the painting.

peach roses

LOUISE JACKSON, MDA

I T HARDLY SEEMS POSSIBLE that the DAC is celebrating its 25th year. It is very exciting to participate in judging the DAC Awards pieces because of the originality that is expressed by the artists. The talent and creativity of decorative artists is amazing. It is expressed beautifully in this program. Our wonderful museum collection has grown under the direction of many people with varied interests. This has created a body of work that exemplifies the true creative aspect of our art form. While we treasure our heritage by collecting many old pieces, we also honor the contemporary ideas by collecting many different styles that the decorative artists of today are creating.

This watercolor of two roses is pretty easy to paint. It is a simple impression of some lovely, fresh garden roses. I hope you enjoy it.

MATERIALS

BRUSHES
Royal Langnickel Majestic synthetics:
- no. 12 round
- no. 20 flat bright
- 1-inch (25mm) flat
- Soft scrubber #170
- Stiff scrubber #475

MAIMERI-BLU WATERCOLORS
Primary Yellow, Rose Lake, Verzino Violet, Permanent Violet Reddish, Cobalt Blue, Faience Blue.

ADDITIONAL MATERIALS
Winsor & Newton Art Masking Fluid
Rubber cement pick-up (to remove the masking fluid)

SURFACE
11 x 15-inch (27.9 x 38.1 cm) Winsor & Newton 300 lb. cold press watercolor paper

This pattern may be hand-traced or photocopied. Enlarge at 200%, then enlarge at 111% to bring up to full size.

PREPARATION

Trace the pattern on with wax-free graphite paper. Make marks dark or they will be lost. Be sure to trace the dotted lines and "X"s.

Carefully apply art masking fluid on the areas that are marked with an "X" on the pattern at left. Straight outer lines means less correcting later. Apply the masking fluid with an old brush that has been dipped in water and coated with regular bar soap. Wipe the excess on a paper towel. You must clean the brush and start again about every five minutes. Apply dots of masking in the flower centers. Let these be ragged and irregular in size.

PALETTE

Mix two wells of color, one for Rose Lake and one for Verzino Violet. Add half of a small pea size to 1 tablespoon of water in each. The color should look like a middle value. Your palette will also contain these colors:

Primary Yellow: strong mix
Cobalt Blue: medium value
Faience Blue + thick Primary Yellow:
    dark blue-green
Faience Blue: light value

PAPER

Tape your paper to a support. Press the tape down so it is tight. Wet the entire paper by dipping your hand into the water and placing lots of water on the paper. When the paper is soaked, pour off the excess toward each corner. This will keep the edges wet.

1. FIRST COLOR WASHES

Use a 1-inch (25mm) flat and apply Primary Yellow to the top of each flower. Apply Rose Lake to the bottom petals. Apply the Verzino Violet to a few of the petals on the right to begin to separate petals. Apply Cobalt Blue in the upper portion of the background. Apply Faience Blue to the sides and bottom.

Use the dark blue-green mix to paint in some swooping strokes and some grasses on the bottom. Sprinkle salt by rolling it between your fingers and allowing it to hit the paper. The salt will absorb small spots of color and leave white spaces. Dry the paper until it is bone dry. Brush off the salt. The colors remaining on the dry paper are your base. Clean up any edges on the petals with the soft scrubber as needed. Wet the brush and loosen the pigment, then blot with a paper towel.

2. PETALS AND LEAVES

Separate the petals by wetting one and applying stronger Verzino Violet to the deep areas and between some of the petals. When working over yellow, use a stronger mix of Rose Lake to work over yellow. Also paint this mix on some petals of the lower flower for variety, even if there is no yellow. Avoid creating an outline. Rinse and remove all of the water from the no. 12 round, flatten it between your fingers. Fan the brush out and use it to pull out the edge of color. This will blend the transition lines and not create new ones.

Apply Primary Yellow on the entire center. Dab in a drier mix of Rose Lake and Primary Yellow mixed to orange to break up some of the light shapes. Add in a few dots of Permanent Violet Reddish for the darkest value.

Paint in some darker swooping strokes as well as some more grass and leaf shapes with the dark blue-green mix. I kept the leaves very simple since they are filler. Paint a leaf shape with a medium value of the blue-green mix. Lift out a center vein with the chisel edge of the damp no. 20 flat. If you want more detail, use opaque white mixed with the colors and add as much detail as you like.

3. DARK VALUES, BACKGROUND, TRANSITIONS

Paint the darkest values with Rose Lake. On occasion add a bit of Permanent Violet Reddish. When the petals are completely dry you may wet them one at a time and apply the darkest values. Apply the color into the deepest recesses as shown above. Blend as before. Dry the paper. Remove the masking.

4. PETALS, BACKGROUND, FINAL DETAILS

Paint the white rolled petals by wetting the roll and applying the color along the inner edge of the petal. Refer to the illustration for step 2. Leave the outside white. Use the violet on some and the red on some.

Apply another layer to the background. Wet the top section around the rose. Apply a thin wash of both blues. Use the Cobalt Blue to the left and the Faience Blue to the right. Bring the color to the edge of the rose on the right as a middle value. Repeat this on the other sections using only the Faience Blue. Deepen the right side of the paper with a middle value blue. Dry the paper.

Remove the masking and scrub the transition lines with a stiff scrubber so the change between the white and color is more gradual. Apply water to soften the pigment for a minute before scrubbing. Blot with a paper towel, then brush off any paper that loosens. On the outer petals some of the background may bleed on to the flower, which is fine as long as there is no transition line. Dry and burnish the paper with the cut end of the scrubber. Press hard on the paper and make little circles to restore the paper.

tole strokes

JO SONJA JANSEN, MDA

I LOVE TO PAINT, and folk art is a passion of mine. It has been my pleasure to share this love of painting with others for a very long time. As the years have progressed, the realization that we must preserve and record the events and history of our renewed interest in decorative art became most evident. Certainly we will be studied in the future with curious interest as to why so many of us chose to make decorative art our joy.

Congratulations to the DAC on 25 years of recording our journey. Best wishes and our full support for your continuation!

MATERIALS

BRUSHES
Jo Sonja Sure Touch:
- nos. 3 and 4 rounds for basic painting
- no. 2 liner for fine details and stripes
- 1-inch (25mm) flat or oval glaze for applying antiquing color
- 1-inch (25mm) mop or bristle blender for blending out antiquing color

JO SONJA ARTIST'S GOUACHE
Purple Madder, Napthol Crimson, Rose Pink, Gold Oxide, Vermillion, Yellow Deep, Moss Green, Brilliant Green, Raindrop, Ultramarine Blue, Carbon Black, Titanium White, Vellum, Wild Grape

ADDITIONAL MATERIALS
- Retarder or Gel Retarder
- Magic Mix painting medium
- Water-based polyurethane varnish

SURFACE
Old metal teapot with wooden handles

Please repeat
on this side.

center

These patterns may be hand-traced or photocopied. They are shown here full size.

PREPARATION
Prepare the metal teapot by cleaning and wiping dry. Paint the background with Vellum. The green trim is a brush mix of Brilliant Green + Ultramarine Blue + a touch of Titanium White. Paint the blue trim with Raindrop. The violet stripe is Wild Grape or a medium violet mix.

1. BLUE STRIPES
Base the stripes with color wash strokes of Ultramarine Blue. Highlight with watery strokes of Titanium White.

After antiquing, retouch the highlights with watery strokes of Titanium White.

2. VIOLET STRIPES
Paint diagonal violet stripes then decorate with strokes of Vermillion + Titanium White.

3. FLOWERS
Base the roses with Rose Pink. Base the daisy and the small side blossom with Gold Oxide. Base the tulip with Ultramarine Blue.

Base the leaves with Brilliant Green + a touch of Carbon Black. Shade and detail with Purple Madder. Highlight with Napthol Crimson + Vermillion + Titanium White.

You may add additional highlights with the above mix + more Titanium White.

Highlight the daisy and small side blossom first with Gold Oxide + Yellow Deep, then with the previous mix + Titanium White.

Highlight the tulip with Ultramarine Blue + Titanium White. You could use some Raindrop if desired.

The pollen dots are Yellow Deep.

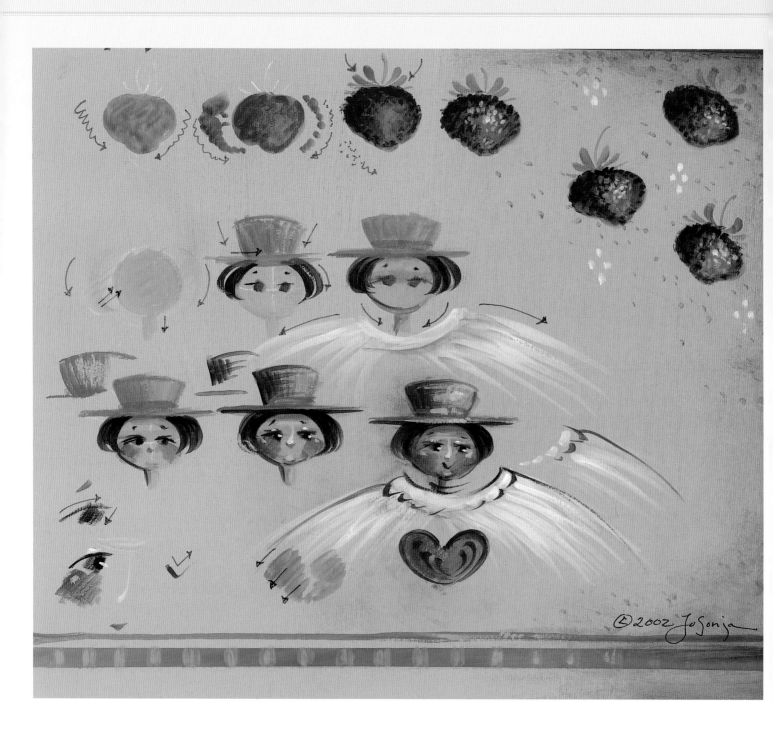

4. STRAWBERRIES

Base with a color wash of Vermillion.

Shade with a dabby color wash of Napthol Crimson.

Darker shading is dabbed on with Purple Madder.

Highlight with dabs of Vermillion + Titanium White.

Final highlights are dabs of Titanium White.

The hulls are strokes of Brilliant Green + a touch of Ultramarine Blue.

Add decorative dots of Titanium White after antiquing.

5. GUARDIAN ANGEL

Base the face and neck with Titanium White + Gold Oxide.

Base the hat with Gold Oxide + Yellow Deep.

Base the eyes and hair with watery strokes of Purple Madder.

Base the wings with watery strokes of Titanium White.

Base the ribbons with Ultramarine Blue and shade the wings with watery Ultramarine Blue.

Shade the hat with toned strokes of Gold Oxide. Continue shading with smaller strokes of Purple Madder.

Paint the pupils of the eyes with Carbon Black.

Shade the hair with some smaller strokes of Carbon Black.

Blush the cheeks with watery strokes of Napthol Crimson + Vermillion. You may also add a touch of blush color to the tip of the nose and the bottom of the chin.

Place Napthol Crimson strokes for lips.

The nose is made with a small stroke of Titanium White highlights.

Highlight the ribbon on the hat with Ultramarine Blue + Titanium White.

6. PINK HEART

The pink heart is based with Napthol Crimson + Titanium White or Rose Pink. Overstroke with Napthol Crimson + Purple Madder.

7. ANTIQUING AND FINISHING

Lightly antique the blue and green areas with Ultramarine Blue + a touch of Brilliant Green and Carbon Black.

Lightly antique the Vellum areas with Brilliant Green + a touch of Carbon Black or Purple Madder. Dry well.

Finish with three to four coats of a water-based polyurethane varnish. Let each coat dry before applying the next.

bird and berries

ANDY B. JONES, CDA

Whirlwind When Designing a Piece To Celebrate the 25th anniversary of the DAC, I wanted something to reflect the history of decorative painting which is so very important. I chose an antique candle box as my surface and I painted it in the style of Peter Ompir who was a tremendously influential decorative artist. I couldn't resist painting strawberries. When I began my decorative painting classes, the first things we painted were strawberries. I added the bird as it was one of the more popular Ompir motifs.

So, happy anniversary to the DAC—here is my twist on history!

MATERIALS

BRUSHES
Silver Brush Ltd.:
- nos. 8, 10 and 12 Golden Natural Flat shaders
- no. 6 Golden Natural Liner
- no. 2 Golden Natural Script Liner
- nos. 4, 6 or 8 Ruby Satin Filberts

FOLKART ARTISTS' PIGMENTS
Titanium White, Warm White, Yellow Light, Sap Green, Burnt Umber, Red Light, Pure Black, True Burgundy, Yellow Ochre, Asphaltum, Burnt Sienna

FOLKART ACRYLICS
Linen, Lipstick Red, Forest Moss

ADDITIONAL MATERIALS
- Water basin
- Paper towels
- Palette knife
- Sepia watercolor
- Oil-based polyurethane varnish
- Varnish brush
- Old facecloth
- Small container with tight fitting lid

SURFACE
Antique wooden candle box

PREPARATION
The candle box was base coated with a 1:1 mixture of Forest Moss and Linen. The bottom edge was trimmed with Forest Moss.

These patterns may be hand-traced or photocopied. Enlarge at 143% to bring up to full size.

1. BASE STRAWBERRIES AND BIRD

For the strawberries, undercoat the leaves with Sap Green +
Burnt Umber. The berries are undercoated with Lipstick Red.
Let dry.

Undercoat the bird with Yellow Ochre. Let dry.

2. SHADE STRAWBERRIES AND BIRD

Shade the berries with a side loaded brush of True Burgundy
and Sap Green (this will make a very dark burgundy).

Shade the bird with Asphaltum and then with Burnt Umber.

ANTIQUE THE PIECE

Step 1: In a small container with a tight fitting lid, squirt a nickle-size dab of sepia watercolor.

Step 2: Dip a wash brush into some water and use the wet brush to thin the watercolor to a syrupy consistency. The paint should not be too thin or runny.

Step 3: Brush the watercolor over the painted design. The design should faintly show through the antiquing syrup. If you can clearly see the design, your antiquing syrup is too thin. Add more watercolor and reapply the mixture to the surface.

Let the mixture dry. The watercolor is not permanent and can be removed without damaging the painting.

Step 4: Wet a facecloth and wring it out thoroughly. If you can't wring it out very well, wrap it in a dry towel and wring it out that way. You want the cloth to be damp, but not wet.

If the cloth is too wet, you will wash off all of the antiquing. If it is too dry you will have a difficult time removing the antiquing. Getting the cloth to have just the right amount of moisture is the most difficult part of the whole process.

Step 5: Fold the facecloth into a soft pad and begin to rub the painting to remove some of the antiquing and make the design more visible.

Now, fold the cloth around your finger and begin to rub on the highlighted areas of the design. Leave the antiquing heavier in the shaded areas of the design.

Be sure to leave the antiquing heavier at the edges of the painting or in crevasses.

As you remove the antiquing, be sure to move to a clean spot on the cloth in order to not redeposit the antiquing in any area where it isn't wanted. If you are unhappy with the antiquing, simply reapply the watercolor and start again.

It may take a couple of tries to get comfortable with this type of antiquing, but it gives an Ompir-like look to the piece.

You should notice where the antiquing has collected in the recesses of the piece and in the brush marks in the background color.

Once you are happy with the antiquing, apply a thin coat of ***oil-based*** polyurethane varnish. Let dry.

3. HIGHLIGHT STRAWBERRIES AND BIRD

The light leaves are highlighted with Sap Green + Yellow Light. Continue to add more yellow and finally a little Titanium White for the final highlights.

Highlight the berries with Red Light. Then, continue the highlights with Red Light + Yellow Light. You want to make sure the berries' highlights are quite yellow.

Highlight the bird with a little Yellow Light and then add small amounts of Titanium White to the brush as you build more highlights. Let dry completely.

4. REFRESH DESIGN AND ADD DETAILS

After antiquing you are going to refresh the design and add additional detail to the painting. Do not repaint the design!

Refresh the highlights on the bird with a little Yellow Light + Titanium White. Add feet with Pure Black. The eye also is Pure Black. The beak is Warm White + Pure Black + a tad of Burnt Umber. Highlight the beak with the undercoat color + more Warm White. Apply a little dabby wash of Red Light and Lipstick Red. Add the dots on the breast. Paint the markings on the wing with Burnt Umber + Pure Black.

To the strawberries, apply leaf veins with Sap Green + Yellow Light + a tad of Titanium White. The stems and tendrils are painted with Burnt Umber. They are highlighted with Burnt Sienna and then with a little Burnt Sienna + Warm White.

Add seeds of Pure Black and Yellow Light. Some additional seeds of Yellow Light + Titanium White will finish the berries.

The bracts are painted with Sap Green + Yellow Light + Burnt Umber. Highlight the bracts with the above mixture + more Yellow Light + a tad of White.

Varnish with a satin sheen oil-based polyurethane varnish.

yesterday's dreams

MARY JO LEISURE, MDA

WHAT A JOY TO BE A PART of the Decorative Arts Collection from its very beginning, to be a part of the dreams of a very few people. Now, 25 years later, the joy is greater as I see and enjoy the beautiful collection that tells a story and captures a part of the journey of decorative painting. With love, care and protection, the journey will continue informing, teaching and showing others what this beautiful art form is all about. I am so proud to be a part of those making this journey.

To me decorative painting is a living art form. I am inspired by everything around me. When I came across this piece in an antique store I knew I needed to paint it. So what is more fitting than white roses and snowberries clustered on all sides, encircling time? I hope you will enjoy sharing my journey. I wish for each of you the excitement of painting.

MATERIALS

BRUSHES
Bette Byrd:
- nos. 2, 4, and 8 flats
- no. 1 round liner

REMBRANDT OIL COLORS
Lemon Yellow, Yellow Ochre, Raw Sienna, Ivory Black, Titanium White, Prussian Blue

WINSOR & NEWTON OIL COLORS
Alizarin Crimson

ADDITIONAL MATERIALS
Liberty Matte Spray finish

SURFACE
Antique clock in wooden box

NOTES ON TECHNIQUE

Work on top objects first, then move toward the background. Create movement in the painting through the use of lost and found edges. Have a balance of warm and cool temperatures in the painting. Use line work to carry your eye through the design. Brush mix colors and spray dry between stages.

Symbols used in the instructions:

+ = Pick up colors together on the brush and mix on the palette.

- = Dry-wipe the brush on a paper towel before picking up the next color.

Throughout the project, the word "mix" before a color means the dirty brush or the last mixture used. The success of your colors depends on using a dirty, dry-wiped brush. Do not clean your brush with thinner between colors.

These patterns may be hand-traced or photocopied. Enlarge the top pattern at 125% and the bottom pattern at 133% to bring them up to full size.

1. SHAPE THE ROSE

These are white roses. To keep variety and interest, vary your values depending on the position in the design. Create accents and tints of color. Your beginning stages should be dark and dull in order for the light areas to set up and take beautiful shape. Using a flat brush and a small amount of color, "fluff" in the shape of the rose with the following colors: Raw Sienna + Black at the bottom of the rose; as you move up, add Yellow Ochre to this mix and then at the top of the rose, add a warm green made from Black + Lemon Yellow.

While this "fluff" is wet, add the overstrokes and work the petals from the back of the outside edge to the tight inside bud. Make as many rows of petals as it takes to fill in the area. Load the brush with Yellow Ochre, Raw Sienna, and then White.

2. BEGIN ROWS OF FRONT PETALS

Using the same procedure of loading the brush, begin to form the bowl of the rose, starting on the inside and working toward the outside. Make as many rows of petals as necessary to complete the bowl of the rose.

3. BEGIN OUTER PETALS

Begin to form petals which will wrap round the bowl. Load the brush in the same manner, but use less White.

Start at the top right, then the top left. Wrap each subsequent petal under the petal above until the area is filled in. Spray dry using Liberty Matte spray.

4. DETAIL THE ROSES

On the dry rose, you will begin to detail the rose and make it come to life. When detailing the rose, first establish the darks. On a dark background be sure your darks are the same value as the background.

The objective is to refine and make the painting vibrant. Do not repaint, just enhance the flower.

Shade: Mix + Black + a scant amount of the dark green mix + Alizarin Crimson.

Highlight: Mix + tiny amounts of Yellow Ochre, Lemon Yellow, Warm Green + White - White.

Tint: Warm Greens, Yellow Ochre, Black + White. You may choose to add tiny amounts of Alizarin Crimson, dark greens, White.

Accent: Yellow Ochre, Raw Sienna.

Add pollen to the center of the rose by dotting in Raw Sienna and Lemon Yellow.

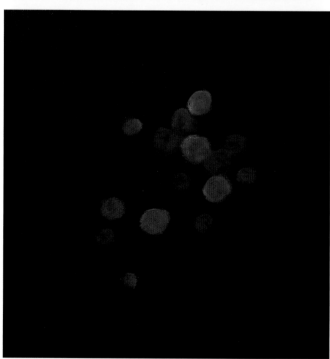

5. BASE THE SNOWBERRIES

Basecoat the berries using a small flat brush and mixture of Black + White + a touch of Alizarin Crimson or the green mixtures so all of the berries are not the same color.

Vary the value of the berries depending on their position in the design. Spray dry the berries with Liberty Matte spray.

6. SHADE AND HIGHLIGHT BERRIES

Shade the dry berries using a very small amount of paint. Use Black to create the dark areas of the berries.

The highlights are Black + White. Add tiny amounts of any of the following colors to create variety in the berries: Alizarin Crimson, Green mixtures, Raw Sienna, and Yellow Ochre.

All stems and line work are added last using the liner brush and green mixtures close to the background value. Highlight the stems with a lighter, warmer green.

7. BASE THE LEAVES

Basecoat the leaves with a mixture of Black + Lemon Yellow + White, if desired.

Be sure to vary the color and value of the green depending on the placement of the leaves in relation to their position in the design.

Spray the leaves dry.

8. SHADE AND HIGHLIGHT

Shade the leaves using very little paint on the dry surface. Use the undercoat mix + Black + a very tiny amount of Prussian Blue.

Highlight the leaves with the green mix + a bit of Lemon Yellow, if desired + White. Add yellow for the warmer leaves and eliminate it for cooler leaves.

9. FINAL HIGHLIGHTS AND TINTS

Add some additional highlights to the leaves and add tints of Yellow Ochre – Black + White and accents of Yellow Ochre. The veins are painted with various shades of green on the chisel edge of the brush. All stems and linework are added last using the liner brush and green mixtures close to the background value. Highlight the stems with a lighter, warmer green.

strokework freesia

MAUREEN McNAUGHTON, MDA, TDA

STROKEWORK IS A STYLE OF DECORATIVE PAINTING that is easily mastered with just a little practice. It is a technique that has been handed down through the ages from painter to painter, and it has been a very important part of our history. As the DAC celebrates its 25th anniversary, I know we are all grateful to them for preserving our past and for their diligence in promoting decorative painting, which assures our future.

MATERIALS

BRUSHES
Maureen McNaughton:
- nos. 1, 3, 5, and 9 round
- nos. 0 and 5/0 liner
- no. 14 and 1-inch (25mm) flat
- no. 1 and 3/4-inch (19mm) mop
- no. 6 Series 200 Pro Round

DECOART AMERICANA ACRYLICS
Antique Gold, Antique White, Antique Rose, Arbor Green, Blue Grey Mist, Buttermilk, Camel, Celery Green, Charcoal Grey, Cranberry Wine, Dove Grey, Dried Basil Green, Driftwood, Honey Brown, Midnite Green, Mink Tan, Neutral Grey, Payne's Grey, Red Violet, Sable Brown, Sand, Shale Green

COLOR MIXES
- *Background colors:* Light Grey = Dove Grey + Driftwood 1:1; Greyed Green = Arbor Green + Charcoal Grey 3:2
- *Medium Yellow:* Camel + Mink Tan + Honey Brown 2:1:1
- *Medium Green:* Dried Basil Green + Charcoal Grey 2:1
- *Medium Cool Green:* Arbor Green + Shale Green 2:1
- *Medium Grey:* Shale Green + Neutral Grey 1:1
- *Dark Violet:* Payne's Grey + Red Violet 1:1 + a touch of Charcoal Grey to dull

ADDITIONAL MATERIALS
- *DecoArt:* Easy Float, Traditions Glazing Medium, Traditions Satin Varnish
- *Krylon:* 18K Gold Leafing pen, Matte Spray #1311
- Chalk
- Light and dark graphite paper
- Dawn Leaf and gold leaf adhesive
- Old brush
- Plastic wrap
- Wet palette

SURFACE
Box #108 from Coyote Woodworks
(705) 865-1414
www.coyotewoodworks.ca

This pattern may be hand-traced or photocopied. Enlarge at 154% to bring up to full size.

Trace the pattern on tracing paper. On the back of the pattern, rub chalk over the dotted arrows. Position the pattern and tape in place. Go over the chalked arrows with a stylus tool. Slip dark graphite paper under the pattern and trace over remaining pattern lines.

PREPARATION

Use a 1-inch (25mm) flat to basecoat the lid with the Light Grey mix. Basecoat the bottom of the box with the Greyed Green mix. Let dry. Sand and tack.

Make extender from distilled water + DecoArt Easy Float 3:1. Add 1-3 drops of extender to a 1-inch (25mm) puddle of each color.

The bottom of the box has the following simple faux finish. Thin Midnite Green with extender. Brush extender over the surface, then the diluted color. Immediately lay plastic wrap loosely over the wet surface. Push into wrinkles with your fingers. Lift and discard the plastic.

Glazing is the very sheer application of transparent color over a damp surface. We will do glazing at the beginning and end of this project.

Glazing Technique: Thin the color with extender so it is transparent. Brush extender over the surface with a large flat, working it into the pores of the surface. The surface should appear evenly moistened with no puddles. Brush the diluted color very sheerly in the desired area with a flat or filbert that is the appropriate size for the area. Immediately, lightly dust the surface with the bristle tips of the dry mop brush to soften and diffuse the color. When dry, you can repeat the process to build the depth of color.

Glaze Blue Grey Mist in from the straight sides of the fan. When dry, apply Glazing Medium that has been thinned with water, as a protective barrier coat.

LOADING THE BRUSH

My technique involves loading the brush in one color and tipping into a contrasting hue. This produces a stroke with soft streaks that resembles the growth direction lines in petals and leaves. If your strokes are too transparent, apply two coats.

1. Dampen the brush. Shake moisture from the ferrule and blot the bristles dry on a soft paper towel.

2. With firm pressure, pull color out from the edge of the puddle to create a loading zone on the palette. Turn the brush over and continue with firm pressure on the other side. Fill the entire length of the bristles with color to allow the brush to open fully in the brushstroke. Shape the brush by pulling all sides lightly through the loading zone again, this time with no pressure on the brush. Do not roll or twist the brush; this will prevent the brush from fanning open during the execution of the stroke.

3. Tipping the brush into a second color. Remove the loading color from the brush tip by drawing it across the sharp edge of the palette. With the handle pointing straight up to the ceiling, dip and stir the tip into a contrasting color—shallow for a small stroke, deeper for a large stroke. Blot the tip gently on the palette to disperse the tipping color up into the brush. Reload for every stroke.

BRUSHSTROKES USED IN THIS PROJECT

Pointed Comma Stroke: Pull a small point, then gradually apply pressure while pulling the brush in a straight or curved path. Halfway through the stroke, gradually release pressure. Slide on the brush tip to form the tail of the stroke.

Pointed Comma Stroke with Long Point/Quick Pressure: Pull a line with the brush tip, then quickly apply pressure while fanning the brush out to the left or right. Pull the brush while gradually releasing pressure. Taper and pull to a fine point.

Comma Stroke: Apply pressure and hesitate to allow the brush bristles to open. Pull in a curved or straight path. Pull and taper to a sharp point.

NOTE: When the stroke is dry, use the liner to pull lines of loading color into the stroke from the point where it finished.

1. LEAVES

Leaves are shown on the pattern with solid head arrows. Form the leaves with pointed comma strokes pulled from the ground to the tip. Use just one coat to avoid texture.

The dotted line arrows represent the background leaves. Load the no. 5 round in Shale Green and tip in Medium Grey. Pull in the small leaf above the open flower. Use the no. 9 round for the remaining background leaves. Go right over any flowers, etc.

2. WARM AND COOL LEAVES

Warm leaves: Load the no. 9 round in Celery Green and tip very shallowly in Charcoal Grey.

Cool leaves: Load the no. 9 round in Medium Cool Green and tip deeply in Midnite Green.

Position the pattern and with light graphite trace on the flowers where they rest over the leaves.

3. VEINS

Brush mix Antique Rose + Mink Tan on the no. 0 liner for the vein in the warm leaves. Vein the cool leaves with Honey Brown. Highlight some veins with a thin line of Camel. Shade all veins in the dark base of the leaf with Cranberry Wine.

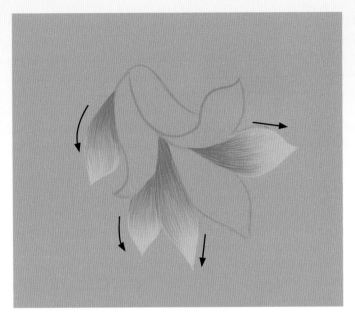

4. OPEN FLOWER AND BUDS

Form the petals in the order indicated on the pattern. When the stroke is dry, sharpen the outer points with the tipping color and pull lines of loading color into the stroke from where it finished.

Load the no. 5 round in Sable Brown and tip in Antique White. Do the three #1 petals with a pointed comma stroke pulled back from the outer tip.

5. OPEN FLOWER AND BUDS

Float Cranberry Wine in the dark base of the #1 petals with the no. 14 flat. Blot the faint edge of the float with the mop brush if required to soften the transition.

6. OPEN FLOWER AND BUDS

Float Antique Rose in the dark base of the #2 petal with the no. 14 flat.

Load the no. 5 round in Camel, tip in Honey Brown. Form the #3 petal with a pressure stroke pulled down into the stem. Also form the dark bud petals with a comma-like stroke pulled back to the stem.

7. OPEN FLOWER AND BUDS

When dry, float Cranberry Wine along the top of the #3 petal.

Mix Cranberry Wine + extender on the no. 5/0 liner. Pull a vein in petals #1 and #2.

Load the no. 5 round in Medium Yellow, tip in Buttermilk. Form the #4 petals with pointed comma strokes pulled back from the outer tips.

Load the no. 5 round in Honey Brown, tip in Sand. Form the light petal in the buds with a comma-like stroke pulled back to the stem.

8. TURNED EDGES ON PETALS

Form the turned edges on the petals with a pointed comma stroke with long point/quick pressure.

Load the no. 1 round in Honey Brown, tip deeply in Sand for the turned edge on the #1 petals.

Do the turned edge on the #2 petal with the no. 1 round loaded in Camel, tipped deeply in Buttermilk.

Form the turned edge on the left #4 petals with the no. 1 round loaded in Sand and tipped deeply in Mink Tan.

Brush mix Camel + Antique Rose in the 5/0 liner and pull lines out from the dark end of the #4 petal and the light bud petal.

9. LEAVES, SEPALS AND VEINS

Use the liner and the tipping color to extend that outer tip of the turned edge to a fine line. Pull lines of loading color out from the tail.

On the turned edge on the left #4 petal, use the 5/0 liner and Sand to extend the tail to line the inside edge of petal #3. Line the valley at the dark end of the turn with a brush mix of Sable Brown + a touch of Antique Rose.

Load the no. 3 round in Dried Basil Green and tip very shallowly in Charcoal Grey. Form the sepals on the buds, the open flower and also the small leaves with pointed comma strokes pulled out from the stem.

Brush-mix Antique Rose plus Mink Tan on the 5/0 liner for the veins in the small leaves, and shade with Cranberry Wine.

Refer to the finished project on page 82 and use the liner for the following:

Fill in the branches with Medium Green. Shade with lines of Charcoal Grey. Highlight with lines of Dried Basil Green and Camel.

Brush mix Mink Tan plus Antique Rose and pull in the tendril. Accent where the tendril crosses over the branch with a line of Cranberry Wine + a touch of Antique Rose.

GLAZING

Thin the Glazing Medium with water and brush it over the lid for a protective barrier coat. Allow to dry.

Glaze Antique Gold in from the upper left in a very thin transparent layer. Apply one coat of diluted Glazing Medium.

When dry, repeat the process with Dark Violet in the lower corners of the fan and up along the sides.

FINISHING

Remove all traces of graphite. In a well ventilated location, wear a mask and spray the lid with several coats of Krylon Matte Finish #1311.

Refer to the photo of the finished project on page 82 for the following instructions. Run the 18K Gold Leafing Pen along the straight sides and rounded top of the lid. If there are cracks in the following gold leaf, the gold pen underneath will hide it. Use an old brush to apply gold leaf adhesive over the pen lines and also in the fancy cutwork edge on the lid and box base. Tear the Dawn Leaf into pieces and lay them over the sized areas. Burnish the leaf and poke it into the holes of the cutwork edge with the no. 6 Series 200 Pro Round brush.

Brush several coats of Traditions Satin Varnish on all surfaces of the box base, the back of the lid and over the gold leaf areas on the lid. Glue a small embellishment on the lid to hide the screw which allows the lid to pivot. I found the small gold shell at a scrapbooking store.

reflections in green and gold

SHERRY C. NELSON, MDA, TDA

I T'S AN HONOR TO BE ASKED to contribute to this milestone publication marking the 25th anniversary of the DAC. I was fortunate to be serving on the Board of Directors of the National Society of Tole and Decorative Painters (now SDP) when the seminal decisions about the founding of the Decorative Arts Collection were made. Thus I have had a heartfelt interest in this worthy organization from its beginning. Painting fruit on rich, dark backgrounds with vibrant, lustrous color is a hallmark of early painting styles. I felt that this piece would be a lovely addition to the Decorative Arts Collection, a modern interpretation of a much-loved traditional look. Adding spectacular reflections to a still life painting doubles the drama and excitement of the piece. And for all their beauty, reflections are one of the easiest special effects to attain. My best wishes to the Board of the DAC for many more years of success in all their endeavors.

MATERIAALS

BRUSHES
Sherry C. Nelson:
- nos. 2, 4, 6 and 8 brights, series 303
- nos. 0 and 1 rounds, series 312

WINSOR & NEWTON ARTISTS' OILS:
Titanium White (W), Raw Sienna (RS), Raw Umber (RU), Sap Green (SG), Cadmium Lemon (CL), Cadmium Yellow Pale (CYP), Cadmium Yellow (CY), Cadmium Orange (CO), Cadmium Scarlet (CS), Alizarin Crimson (AC)

DELTA CERAMCOAT ACRYLICS
Black, Red Iron Oxide

ADDITIONAL MATERIALS
- Cobalt Drier (siccative)
- Odorless thinner
- Graphite transfer paper
- Cheesecloth
- Liberty Matte Finish spray
- Krylon Crystal Clear spray

SURFACE
13 x 9-inch (33 x 22.9 cm) Lemon and Fruit Tray #554 from Mary Ellerman at R & M What Knots. (206) 542-1592. E-mail: rmary10@attbi.com

91

This pattern may be hand-traced or photocopied. Enlarge at 133% to
bring it up to full size. Transfer this pattern, not the Placement Sheets,
to your prepared surface, using light graphite paper.

PREPARATION

Base the center surface of the tray with
a coat of Black acrylic using a sponge
roller. Allow to dry. Sand well. Rebase
with Black. Let dry.

   If you will be gold leafing the rim of
the tray, base it with two coats of Red
Iron Oxide acrylic, sanding between
coats. Spray the entire tray with Liberty
Matte Finish.

USING THE PLACEMENT SHEETS

Placement Sheet 1 shows the location of
all basecoated areas of color.

   Placement Sheet 2 indicates the location for placement of highlights, as well
as shading and accent colors. Colors
shown on Placement Sheet 2 always go
on top of the basecoat colors shown on
Placement Sheet 1.

   Refer to the Placement Sheets often
for location of colors and mixes while

you are painting. Find the specific
color names and mixes in the **written**
instructions.

   Familiarize yourself with the following
abbreviations: B/ = Basecoat; D/ = Dark;
M/ = Medium; L/ = Light; S/ means
Shade; HL/ and xx's indicate highlights.

   Oil colors are referred to by the first
letter of each word; cross-reference these
to the oil color names in the Materials
list on page 91.

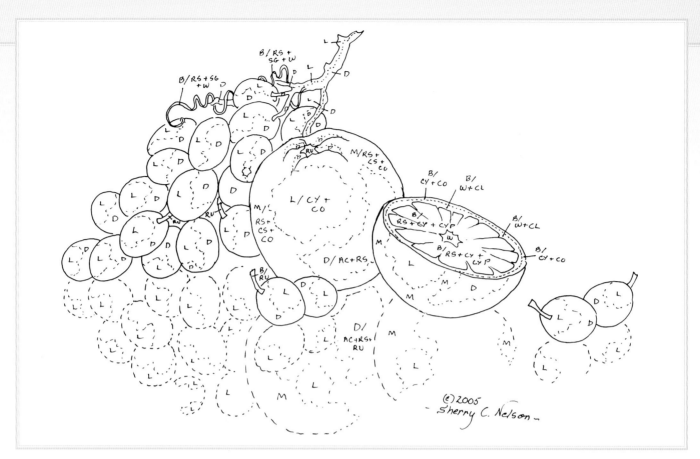

PLACEMENT SHEET 1

PLACEMENT SHEET 2

93

1. ORANGE PEELS

The dark value for the orange peels is Alizarin Crimson + Raw Sienna; medium value is Raw Sienna + Cadmium Scarlet + a little Cadmium Orange; light value is Cadmium Yellow + Cadmium Orange.

Apply these values with the no. 6 bright, using little paint and lots of pressure and chopping on colors in all directions. When all color areas are applied, blend where values meet with the same choppy, multi-directional brushstrokes to achieve a good value gradation.

Apply the first highlight, inside dotted line shown on Placement Sheet 2, using Cadmium Yellow + Cadmium Yellow Pale + Raw Sienna. Blend the edges of this color into basecoat. Now add lighter highlights where xx's indicate, using Cadmium Yellow Pale + Cadmium Lemon. Blend edges again into the basecoat. A final bit of Cadmium Lemon + White can be added for final spark.

On the blossom end of the orange, base with Raw Umber. Highlight with a bit of White or Raw Sienna + White.

2. REFLECTIONS OF ORANGES

For the reflections, use sparse paint and allow the black background to be the dark area in each reflection.

The dark value for the oranges' reflections is the black background; medium value is Raw Sienna + Cadmium Scarlet; light value is Cadmium Orange. Apply sparsely and blend slightly between values with the brush, then use a bit of cheesecloth to soften and subdue colors, removing any excess paint.

Rub out bottom edges to blend with the background. Dampen the no. 8 bright with a little odorless thinner and blot on paper towel. Slice through reflections here and there to create horizontal lines that indicate graining, which creates natural breaks in the reflection.

3. ORANGE HALF

Base just under the peel with Cadmium Yellow + Cadmium Orange. Base the inside peel with White + Cadmium Lemon. Stipple a bit with the chisel edge as you base it to get a little fuzzy texture for more realism.

Base sections of orange with Raw Sienna + Cadmium Yellow + Cadmium Yellow Pale. Soften brushstrokes in natural growth direction of each section, minimizing texture. Then place the light section lines in between a few sections using the Cadmium Lemon + White mix. Widen the outer end of some of the section lines where they join the Cadmium Lemon + White mix previously applied.

Fill in the star-shaped center with White and soften a bit with Raw Sienna + Cadmium Yellow mix.

4. GRAPES

For the grapes the dark value is Raw Umber + Sap Green + White; the light value is dirty brush + Sap Green + White. Lay on values as indicated on Placement Sheet 1, using sparse paint. Blend where values meet, using choppy strokes of the no. 4 bright. Shade with Raw Umber. Place a few discolored areas of Raw Sienna on some grapes for accent.

Highlight the forward-most grapes in the design with a mix of Sap Green + White, placed where indicated by xx's. Blend edges of highlight value slightly to create gradation. Add a spark of Sap Green + more White mix on some dominant grapes. Finally add accent backlighting on grapes where indicated with AA's, using a no. 2 bright, and a mix of Cadmium Yellow + Cadmium Scarlet. Soften edges of accent slightly into basecoat.

5. REFLECTIONS OF GRAPES

The dark value for the grapes' reflections is the black background; light value is a mix of Raw Umber + Sap Green + White, only slightly lighter than the dark value mix used on the grapes themselves. Apply paint sparsely and then blend a bit with brush to break up the edge. Rub a bit with cheesecloth to remove excess paint and to soften into background. Add some subtle smudges of highlight color on a few reflections using a slightly lighter value of Raw Umber + Sap Green + White. Add a few soft smudges of accent color using Cadmium Yellow + Cadmium Scarlet. Rub slightly into background to subdue.

When all reflections are complete, use a clean no. 8 bright dampened in thinner and blotted on paper towel to lift out graining lines in tabletop.

6. STEMS AND TENDRILS

In the large areas of the stem, use Raw Umber for dark value areas and White in light. Where stems are too tiny to divide, base the entire stem with Raw Umber. Blend slightly between values on larger stems, and highlight smaller ones with a bit of dirty White using the chisel of a no. 2 bright.

For the tendril, make a thin mix of Sap Green + Raw Sienna + White. Stroke on tendril with this basecoat, using the no. 1 round brush. Then add a bit more White to the same thinned mix, and overlay this lighter value mix on a few forward curves of the tendril for highlights.

GOLD LEAFING

Wait until the painting is finished and totally dry before you begin gold leafing.

Paint the tray flange using Red Iron Oxide acrylic. Let dry, buff with steel wool, and recoat. Spray with Liberty Matte Finish.

Shake sizing well, and cut the pad of gold leaf into a size that is compatible to the area you plan to leaf, allowing a little extra.

Using a synthetic brush, apply sizing (a glue) to the area to be leafed. Do not leave lumps or ridges of sizing; brush on smoothly and evenly over area to be leafed.

Once all sizing has dried clear, begin to pick up individual pieces of leaf from the cut stack, holding each by the tissue interleaving. Touch down to the sized surface, and using the tissue, pat gently into place. Continue to place leaf onto surface until all sized areas are loosely covered. Then using a pad of cheesecloth, firmly but carefully press the leaf onto the surface.

Allow to dry several hours, then brush off excess leaf (out of doors) using the pad of cheesecloth. Spray with Krylon Crystal Clear to protect from tarnishing and to retain the characteristic shine. Do not use Matte Finish over metal leaf.

When antiquing the leaf I use my Raw Umber oil paint for the antique glaze, mixing it with odorless thinner and a drop of Cobalt Drier until it is very puddly. Brush glaze onto leaf, making sure it gets down into all the crevices of the frame. Then wipe off excess, using the cheesecloth. You may remove most of the glaze for a brighter gold or less for a more antiqued look. Let dry, then spray entire surface, including painting, with a final finish of Krylon Spray Varnish, #7002.

bee kind

MAXINE THOMAS

I APPRECIATE THE OPPORTUNITY TO SHARE a design with you on the 25th anniversary of the Decorative Arts Collection. Art in any form is an expression of who we are individually and as a culture. It is a blessing to have a collection of varied art styles available in the DAC museum. My sincere thanks go to those who contribute and care for this collection, an important part of our creative history.

MATERIALS

BRUSHES
Loew-Cornell:
- 3/8-inch (10mm) stippler
  (for stippling bear)
- 3/8-inch (10mm) crescent
  (for dry-brushing highlights)
- 1/2-inch (13mm) and 3/4-inch
  (19mm) Maxine's Mops
  (for blending)
- no. 12 and 3/4-inch (19mm) flats
  (for floating shades)
- 10/0 liner (for line work)
- nos. 6 and 12 filberts
  (for basecoating)

DECOART AMERICANA ACRYLIC COLORS
Light Buttermilk, Antique White, Khaki Tan, Mississippi Mud, Marigold, Honey Brown, Milk Chocolate, Dark Chocolate, Bittersweet Chocolate, Burnt Orange, Burnt Sienna, Hot Shots Fiery Red, Uniform Blue, Green Mist, Antique Teal, Heritage Brick, Soft Black, Lamp Black

ADDITIONAL MATERIALS
- DecoArt Matte Finishing Spray
- DecoArt Multi-Purpose Sealer
- Permalba Burnt Umber oil paint
  (for antiquing)
- Sanding disk
- Scottie's Patina
  (thinner for antiquing)
- Stylus
- Tracing paper
- Transfer paper

SURFACE
Small lap desk available from:
Smooth Cut Wood
P. O. Box 507
Aurora, OR 97002
phone: 1-888-982-9663

This pattern may be hand-traced or photocopied.
Enlarge at 137% to bring it up to full size.

PREPARATION

Sand and seal the wood piece. Basecoat the design surface with Khaki Tan. The main part of the wood piece (where the pattern is placed) is painted with Honey Brown. Paint the edges and linework words with Lamp Black. The checkered area at top and bottom on the design is basecoated with Lamp Black and stamped with Honey Brown checks. Let dry and transfer the main pattern lines.

1. BASECOAT ALL ELEMENTS

Use an appropriate size filbert brush (no. 6 or 12) and basecoat all the elements in the design as follows:

Crock: Dark Chocolate (stripe and spatter are Antique White).

Left book: Antique Teal.

Right book: Heritage Brick.

Beehive, including stick and flagpole: Milk Chocolate.

Bear: Mississippi Mud. Paint foot patches Antique White.

Flag: Light Buttermilk. Use Uniform Blue for the field of blue, Light Buttermilk for the star and Heritage Brick for the red stripes.

Sign: Light Buttermilk.

Rusty star garland, including wire: Burnt Sienna.

2. SHADING

Apply the shading to the elements of the design using a floated color or a side-loading technique.

Crock: Shade with Soft Black under top rim, down each side (wider next to bear), across bottom and left of flag. Deepen next to bear with Lamp Black.

Beehive: Using a liner or rake brush, stroke back and forth with Honey Brown, then Marigold, keeping strength of highlight to the center. Softly shade down each side with Soft Black. Add some Soft Black tendrils and basecoat the hole. Shade inside hole on right with Lamp Black.

Rusty Star Garland: Dampen stars and dab in Soft Black with the corner of your brush making the rusty texture. When dry, shade with Soft Black on the bottoms of the stars and on the wire on each side of stars.

Flag: Shade with Soft Black on bottom of pole and on flag next to pole. Highlight down pole with Honey Brown, then Marigold.

Books: Shade down each side of each book with Soft Black (stronger behind the bear). Highlight top of green book with Green Mist. Bands are Lamp Black. Highlight down center of red book with Hot Shots Fiery Red. Line words with Lamp Black. Bands are Honey Brown. Shade each side of bands with Burnt Sienna, then Soft Black.

Bittersweet: Line the branches with Soft Black. Dot berries with Heritage Brick and Burnt Orange. Add tiny highlight dots on some with Marigold.

Bear: Stipple all over with Khaki Tan, leaving some of the darker color showing through. Transfer pattern lines and shade with Bittersweet Chocolate (to keep the furry look, float with a choppy stroke rather than pulling a straight line); inside ears, across top of head ear to ear, under ears and down sides of head,

around muzzle (eye to eye), under head, down center of body, down left arm next to body, around left paw on body, left of right arm on chest, under arms on legs, behind feet, outside of foot patches, bottom of patches and softly along bottom of muzzle, down back of arms and heels of feet for shape. Strengthen deeper places with Bittersweet Chocolate again or use Soft Black.

Sign: Shade softly along bottom with Soft Black. Bee body is Marigold. Shade across bottom with Burnt Sienna. Line

words, basecoat bee's head, antennae, stripes, stinger, bee trail, dot holes, line wings and wire with Lamp Black.

Floor: Shade under bear feet and sign with Soft Black. Highlight along top edge with Marigold.

milk. Left patch is Antique Teal. Shade left edge with Soft Black and highlight on right with Green Mist. Eyes, nose stitches, mouth line and paw stitches are Lamp Black. Add Light Buttermilk highlight dots to eyes and nose.

Sign: Skip a Light Buttermilk highlight down the wire.

Floor: Highlight along top edge with Marigold.

FINISHING

Please refer to the photo of the finished project on page 96. The background shading is Dark Chocolate and Soft Black in deeper places. Line where needed with Lamp Black.

ANTIQUING

Please refer to the photo of the finished project on page 96. Using a plastic lid, press out some Burnt Umber oil paint and pour in some thinner. No need to mix them together. Put on rubber gloves and grab an old rag. Dab into both the paint and the thinner and blend them together as you wipe all over your piece. With a clean part of your rag, wipe off the antiquing (especially in the center of design) until it is the soft color you like. To make edges darker, dab into straight oil paint and apply to edges, then soften with a rag to desired shade. Immediately lightly mist with spray acrylic varnish. This will dry the oil quickly. When this light coat is dry, give it one or two good coats of spray varnish. If you are going to brush varnish, you will want to wait a day or two to make sure the oil is dry.

3. HIGHLIGHTS

Crock: Drybrush highlight with Antique White, then Light Buttermilk, on center of rim and down center of crock.

Rusty Star Garland: Highlight with Burnt Orange (dabbing in color to keep rusty texture) on top of each star and here and there along wires.

Flag: Highlight red stripes on flag with Hot Shots Fiery Red, then drybrush a Light Buttermilk highlight.

Books: Highlight the center of the bands with Marigold. Drybrush soft Light Buttermilk highlights down center.

Bear: Stipple highlight (or use a small round and dab in color) with Antique White + Khaki Tan, then Antique White on tops of ears, forehead, center of muzzle, down center of right arm, left edge of left arm, center of paws and tops of feet. Highlight center of paw patches with Light Buttermilk. Basecoat chest patch Light Buttermilk and Uniform Blue. Shade left side, next to arm with Bittersweet Chocolate then Soft Black and highlight at left with Light Butter-

spring floral bag

MARY M. WISEMAN

THE DECORATIVE ARTS COLLECTION is a history of the art form of decorative painting. As we celebrate the 25th anniversary of the DAC, to me it was only fitting to choose a piece that is reflective of our current trends along with the timeless rose that is so indicative of decorative painting. It is my pleasure to create a design to celebrate our anniversary and to be a part of the history of this beautiful art form.

MATERIALS

BRUSHES
Loew-Cornell:
- 1/8-inch (3mm), 1/4-inch (6mm), 3/8-inch (10mm), 1/2-inch (13mm), 5/8-inch (16mm) and 3/4-inch (19mm) Angle Brushes
- 10/0 Liner
- no. 4 Fabric Round
- extra small and small Dome Rounds
- no. 2 Filbert

DELTA CERAMCOAT ACRYLIC COLORS
Antique White, Moss Green

DECOART AMERICANA ACRYLIC COLORS
Black Green, Black Plum, Buttermilk, Cranberry Wine, Dioxazine Purple, Ebony Black, French Vanilla, Light Avocado, Light Buttermilk, Moon Yellow, Pansy Lavender, Plantation Pine, Royal Purple, Taffy Cream, Traditional Burnt Umber, True Ochre

ADDITIONAL MATERIALS
- Stylus
- Tracing paper
- Waxed palette paper
- Wet palette
- Gray or white transfer paper
- J.W.'s Right Step Matte Varnish
- 1-inch (25mm) foam brush
- Fine 220-grit sandpaper
- DecoArt Wood Sealer
- Low tack tape
- Small sea sponge
- Krylon 18 KT Gold Leafing Pen

SURFACE
Wooden handbag available from:
La Maison BeL'Art
Quebec, Canada
phone: (450) 530-2161
www.nvo.com/belarts

These patterns may be hand-traced or
photocopied. Enlarge the main pattern at
135% and the border pattern at 147% to
bring them up to full size.

PREPARATION

Seal the wooden purse using DecoArt Wood Sealer. Apply using a foam brush. When dry, sand using fine 220 grit sandpaper. Tack off the sanding dust using a tack rag.

With a large wash brush or foam brush, basecoat the purse inside and out with Delta Ceramcoat Antique White. When dry, repeat the Antique White for solid coverage. Lightly sand the surface between coats.

The top of the purse and the scallop overhang are based solid using Moss Green. Create a green band that is placed in the center of the bag and goes all the way around the purse by measuring 1-3⁄4 inches (4.4cm) down from the scallop trim and 1-3⁄4 inches (4.4cm) up from the bottom edge of the purse. The band will measure approximately 3 inches (7.6cm) in width; use low tack tape above and below the band to mask. Basecoat the band solidly using Moss Green. When dry, dampen the Moss Green areas with water and, using a wet sea sponge dipped in Antique White, press the sponge into the damp green areas to give a marbleized appearance to the green areas.

Using the Krylon Gold Leafing pen, add a small stripe on the edge of the green band along the top and bottom. Run the pen around the edge of the scalloped area of the overhang.

Paint the ball feet on the bottom of the purse using Moss Green. The six wooden handle spindles are painted Antique White and the center rings are Moss Green. Place a gold ring in the groove on both sides of the Moss Green.

Thin Moss Green with water to an ink-like consistency. Load a round fabric brush with the thinned color and spatter the Antique White areas of the purse.

Trace and transfer the roses and violets pattern onto the center of the green band. Slip transfer paper between the surface and the tracing. Using a stylus, trace on the main lines of the flowers and leaves.

Trace and transfer the strokework border pattern onto the scalloped area of the purse. Load a liner brush with Antique White and paint in the comma strokes and dots.

1. BASECOAT DESIGN

Basecoat the elements of the design. Use a brush size that fits the area. The leaves and violets may require more than one coat to achieve opaque coverage.

Leaves: Mix 1 part Taffy Cream + 1 part Light Avocado.

Violets: Mix 1 part Pansy Lavender + 1 part Buttermilk.

Roses: Basecoat using a wash of Moon Yellow.

2. SHADING AND LIGHT VALUES

Apply shading and light values to the leaves and the violets. Shade areas of the roses.

Leaves: Shade the leaves using a sideload float of Light Avocado on a 1/2-inch (13mm) angle brush. The light values are applied using Taffy Cream and are floated in the areas or dry brushed.

Repeat the Light Avocado for a second shading; the color may slightly float over the light areas to unify the values.

Violets: Using a 3/8-inch (10mm) angle brush, sideload float a shade of Pansy Lavender. Apply a highlight to the light areas using a 3/8-inch (10mm) or a 1/4-inch (6mm) angle brush dressed in the base color and sideloaded with But-

termilk. When the light area is dry, float a second shading using Pansy Lavender + Royal Purple.

Roses: Float shading in the throat area and at the base of the rose bowl using Moon Yellow + a touch of True Ochre. When dry, repeat the float keeping it a little tighter using True Ochre + Dioxazine Purple (6:1).

3. STRENGTHEN SHADING AND HIGHLIGHTS

Strengthen the shade and light areas of the flowers and leaves.

Leaves: Mix a small amount of Dioxazine Purple into Plantation Pine to dull the color slightly. Thin a small amount of the mix with water and load on a liner brush. Line in the center and side veins

of each of the leaves. Using a 1/2-inch (13mm) angle brush, sideload float the mix to deepen the shaded areas of each leaf. Using Taffy Cream + Buttermilk, drybrush to lighten the light area of each leaf.

Violets: Sideload float a second light using a 1/4-inch (6mm) angle brush and Buttermilk on the light areas of the violet petals. Deepen the shade areas of the violets using the same brush sideloaded with Royal Purple.

Roses: The petals are stroked on using an angle brush dressed in French Vanilla and sideloaded in Buttermilk. Start at the back of the rose, then the front of the rose, and finally the skirt petals.

4. FINAL TINTS AND ACCENTS

Add the final shades and highlights, accents and tints to all the elements in the design.

Leaves: The shaded areas of the leaves can be deepened using Black Green + Traditional Burnt Umber on a small angle brush and floated into the triangle areas of the leaves. Accents are floated into the dark to mid-value areas using one or several of the following colors: Cranberry Wine, Black Plum, Dioxazine Purple.

A highlight is drybrushed to the light areas using Buttermilk + Light Buttermilk.

Violets: Deepen the shaded areas using Royal Purple + a touch of Ebony Black. Drybrush a highlight on the petals using Light Buttermilk + Buttermilk. Accent color can be washed on in the middle- to light-value area using Cranberry Wine or Dioxazine Purple.

Place a press dot of Moon Yellow in the "V" area of the largest petal of each violet. Thin Ebony Black + Dioxazine Purple (1:1) with water and load a liner brush with the mix; pull hairlines in the largest petal of each violet. A small comma is stroked on both sides of the Moon Yellow dot using Light Buttermilk

Roses: Sideload float a highlight on each of the light strokes using Buttermilk + Light Buttermilk. Deepen the shaded areas and float in accents behind some of the light petals using Cranberry Wine + Black Plum.

The center of each of the roses has pollen dots scattered using the tip of the liner brush starting with Cranberry Wine + Black Plum, and then True Ochre, Moon Yellow, Buttermilk and finally a few Light Buttermilk.

The vines in the background are Plantation Pine + a touch of Traditional Burnt Umber to cool the color. Thin with water to an ink-like consistency and pull the vines using a liner brush.

The small leaves are painted with a no. 2 filbert using thin Moss Green touched into Light Avocado. The leaves are formed by a press-pull in the desired areas. Pull stems in using Plantation Pine + a touch of Traditional Burnt Umber.

Finish with several coats of J.W's Right Step Matte Varnish or your favorite varnish.

a gallery of treasures
from the DECORATIVE ARTS COLLECTION

ON THE FOLLOWING PAGES is a comprehensive selection of the wide variety of artworks contained in the Decorative Arts Collection as of 2007, the 25th Anniversary of the beginning of the collection. The works range from historic, either in style or time of creation, to contemporary. There is also a selection of artworks that have won the DAC Awards, a juried art competition that seeks the best of contemporary decorative painting. The breadth and scope of the artform is clearly apparent in the photos you are about to see. Enjoy the journey!

the historic collection

THE DECORATIVE ARTS COLLECTION'S historic works provide a foundation for all of the pieces in the collection. These examples show some of the earliest forms of decorative painting done in the United States and in Europe.

There are fine examples of American Country painted tinware, Chippendale painting, Pontypool painting, theorem, calligraphy and others. Many of these works are prime examples and have been studied extensively.

To know that many of the artists who created these works did so under harsh circumstances, with limited or handmade supplies, makes each piece in the historic collection very special… they are the foundation of what contemporary artists do.

PHOTO ALBUM
Artist: unknown
Medium: Oil, mother-of-pearl on wood
Dimensions: 8-1/2 x 7-1/2 inches
   (22 x 19 cm)

THEOREM
Artist: Emeline Adriance
Medium: Watercolor on velvet
Dimensions: 21 x 24 inches
   (53 x 61 cm)

COFFEEPOT WITH "SCRAMBLED EGG" DECORATION
Artist: unknown
Medium: Asphaltum, Japan color on tin
Dimensions: 14 x 7-1/2 inches (36 x 19 cm)

COFFIN CORNER TRAY
Artist: unknown
Medium: Asphaltum, Japan
  color on tin
Dimensions: 8-2/3 x 12-1/2
  inches (22 x 32 cm)

BUN TRAY
Artist: unknown
Medium: Asphaltum, Japan color on tin
Dimensions: 4 x 12 x 3-1/2 inches (10 x
  30 x 9 cm)

111

CALLIGRAPHIC LION
Artist: unknown
Medium: Ink on paper
Dimensions: 17-3⁄4 x 23 inches (45 x 58 cm)

This design of a lion is composed of calligraphic pen strokes. The creation of fanciful animals and birds utilizing penwork was a common outgrowth of the home arts that were taught in schools. Calligraphy or penmanship was taught alongside other crafts such as sewing and needlework. The ability to write beautifully was considered quite important in the late 1700s and early 1800s. The level of skill depicted in this drawing of a lion is quite extraordinary.

GERMAN BRIDE'S BOX
Artist: unknown
Medium: Oil on wood
Dimensions: 18-1/2 x 11 x 5-1/2 inches
(47 x 28 x 13 cm)

TRUNK WITH WHITE BAND
Artist: unknown
Medium: Asphaltum, Japan color on tin
Dimensions: 9-1/2 x 7 x 6 inches
(24 x 18 x 15 cm)

TRUNK WITH WHITE ARCH
Artist: unknown
Medium: Asphaltum, Japan color on tin
Dimensions: 8-1/2 x 6-1/2 x 5 inches
(22 x 17 x 13 cm)

URN OF FLOWERS
Artist: Ellen Sabine
Medium: Oil on glass
Dimensions: 13-1/4 x 10 inches
(33.7 x 25.4 cm)

**CROOKNECK COFFEEPOT WITH
TRADITIONAL DECORATION**
Artist: unknown
Medium: Japan color on tin
Dimensions: 11 x 6 inches (28 x 15 cm)

This stunning example of country painted tinware is the signature piece of the Decorative Arts Collection Museum. Country painted tin, or American painted tin as it is sometimes called, is a style of painting with brushstrokes, popular in America in the 18th and 19th centuries. The objects painted were typically tin, though the style was also used on furniture and wood. Characteristics of the style include pendant brushstrokes, stems added to stylized flowers and leaves, and overstrokes and details painted on the larger objects.

This piece was purchased at auction by the DAC in 1984. It is a prime example of painted tinware made in New England in the 1700s. The red background on this crookneck coffeepot is perhaps the most sought-after color by collectors and museums alike. We are indeed fortunate to have a piece of such historic significance as a part of our collection.

the contemporary collection

I T WAS DETERMINED EARLY IN THE HISTORY of the DAC that contemporary pieces of decorative painting should be saved while they were readily available and affordable. To this end, the trustees have been soliciting works and purchasing work from time to time to build a comprehensive collection of decorative painting that shows a variety of mediums, styles and techniques. The pieces shown on this and the following pages are examples from different decades in the recent past and show the changing styles of painting, color trends and surfaces.

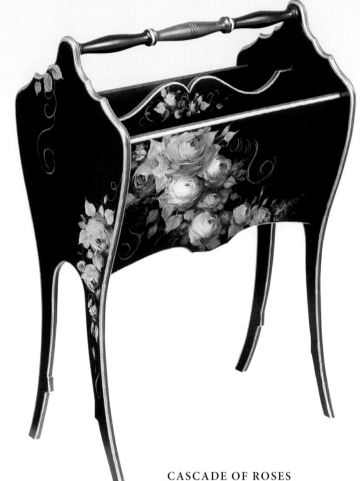

CASCADE OF ROSES
Artist: Trudy Beard
Medium: Acrylic on wood
Dimensions: 7-1⁄2 x 18 x 8-1⁄2 inches
  (19 x 46 x 22 cm)

FLORAL BOX
Artist: Becky Bordelon
Medium: Pen and ink, acrylic on wood
Dimensions: 8 x 6 x 1-1⁄2 inches
  (20 x 15 x 4 cm)

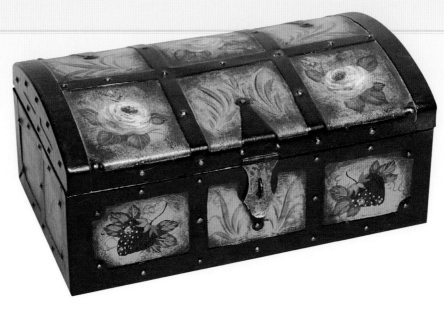

**TRUNK WITH ROSES
AND STRAWBERRIES**
Artist: Robert Berger
Medium: Acrylic on tin
Dimensions: 4 x 10 x 6 inches
   (10 x 25 x 15 cm)

CIDER PITCHER
Artist: Robert Berger
Medium: Acrylic on tin
Dimensions: 20 x 4-1⁄2 inches
   (51 x 11 cm)

KEROSENE CAN
Artist: Robert Berger
Medium: Acrylic on metal
Dimensions: 12 x 9-3⁄4 inches
   (30 x 25 cm)

PORTLAND ROSE
Artist: Susan Scheewe
Medium: Watercolor on paper
Dimensions: 11 x 14 inches
   (28 x 37 cm)

SERENITY
Artist: Brenda Stewart
Medium: Acrylic on porcelain
Dimensions: 8 x 8 inches (20 x 20 cm)

SUMMER SAMPLER
Artist: Betty Caithness
Medium: Acrylic on wood
Dimensions: 11-1/2 x 9 x 4-1/2 inches
   (29 x 23 x 11 cm)

METAL PLATE WITH FOLK ART RABBITS AND CHICKENS
Artist: Terrie Cordray
Medium: Acrylic on metal
Dimensions: 12-1⁄2 inches diameter
   (32 cm)

TRADITIONAL FOLK ART
Artist: Helen Cavin
Medium: Mixed media on wood
Dimensions: 7-3⁄4 x 13 x 6-3⁄4 inches
   (20 x 33 x 17 cm)

APPLE STUDY
Artist: Doris Christoffel
Medium: Acrylic on panel
Dimensions: 8 x 10 inches
   (20 x 25 cm)

ELEGANT TRAY
Artist: Vilma Fabretti
Medium: Oil on wood
Dimensions: 18 x 10 x 1-1⁄2
  inches (46 x 25 x 4 cm)

ROSES
Artist: Lucille DeWitt
Medium: Oil on canvas
Dimensions: 4 x 5 inches
  (10 x 13 cm)

**TIME TO SMELL
THE ROSES**
Artist: Ginger Edwards
Medium: Oil on wood
Dimensions: 7-1⁄2 x 10 x 2-1⁄2
  inches (19 x 25 x 6 cm)

STILL LIFE
Artist: Nadine Farquahar
Medium: Oil on canvas
Dimensions: 10 x 12-3⁄4 inches
   (25 x 32 cm)

EAGLE
Artist: Kathi Chapin
Medium: Oil on slate
Dimensions: 10-1⁄4 x 14 inches
   (26 x 36 cm)

FLORAL BOUQUET
Artist: Dolores Furnari
Medium: Oil on velvet
Dimensions: 11 x 14 inches
   (28 x 36 cm)

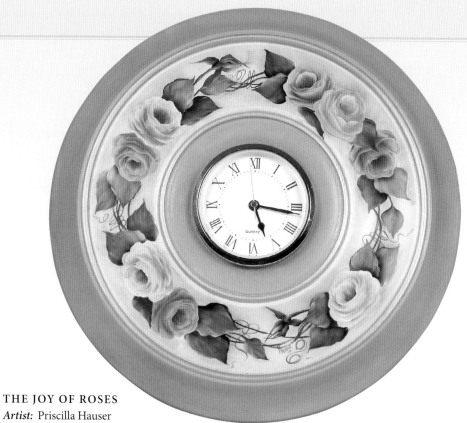

THE JOY OF ROSES
Artist: Priscilla Hauser
Medium: Acrylic on wood
Dimensions: 12-inches diameter (30 cm)

TULIPS
Artist: Mary Lou Garrison
Medium: Oil on wood
Dimensions: 25-1/2 x 5-1/2 inches
    (65 x 14 cm)

SOFT AND SIMPLE
Artist: Mary Lou Garrison
Medium: Watercolor on rice paper
Dimensions: 10 x 13 inches (25 x 33 cm)

LINEN TRAY
Artist: Harmen Glashouwer
Medium: Acrylic on wood
Dimensions: 19-1/2 x 12 x 4 inches
  (50 x 30 x 10 cm)

CLEMATIS
Artist: Peggy Hobbs
Medium: Oil on wood
Dimensions: 13 x 5 inches
  (33 x 13 cm)

BUTTER CHURN AND CROCKS
Artist: Virginia Jarboe
Medium: Oil on wood
Dimensions: 13-3/4 x 8-3/4 inches
  (35 x 22 cm)

ROSES
Artist: Marian Houghton
Medium: Oil on metal
Dimensions: 19-1⁄2 x 13 inches
 (50 x 33 cm)

OLD-FASHIONED ROSES
Artist: Marian Houghton
Medium: Oil on wood
Dimensions: 12 x 12-1⁄2 x 5 inches
 (30 x 32 x 13 cm)

WHITE DAISIES
Artist: Marian Houghton
Medium: Oil on wood
Dimensions: 9-1⁄2 x 17-3⁄4
 inches (24 x 45 cm)

TRAY
Artist: Joyce Howard
Medium: Mixed media on wood
Dimensions: 20 x 12 inches (51 x 30 cm)

ROSES AND RIBBON
Artist: Jean Wortham
Medium: Oil on wood
Dimensions: 8-1/4 x 6-3/4 x 4 inches (21 x 17 x 10 cm)

ANNIVERSARY CLOCK
Artist: Jo Sonja Jansen
Medium: Acrylic gouache on wood
Dimensions: 14 x 8 x 5 inches (36 x 20 x 13 cm)

ROSE MIRROR
Artist: Joan Johnson
Medium: Oil on wood
Dimensions: 17-3/4 inches
    diameter (45 cm)

FRUIT CANISTER—PATTERN OF THE MONTH
Artist: Joan Johnson
Medium: Oil on mylar
Dimensions: 8-1/2 x 11 inches
    (22 x 28 cm)

 # NOTEWORTHY

ROSES
Artist: Joan Johnson
Medium: Oil on metal
Dimensions: 7-1/4 x 10 inches
    (18 x 25 cm)

Joan Johnson, MDA, was a pioneer in the field of contemporary decorative painting. She was one of the first artists to publish patterns and instructions for decorative artists. She published her "Pattern of the Month" for many years. The DAC is proud to have the entire library of the original artwork for these patterns. Joan was one of the original Master Decorative Artists (MDA) designated by the Society of Decorative Painters. She designed the logos for the Society and for the Decorative Arts Collection.

She was very mild mannered and never craved attention, yet her quiet way influenced the path of decorative painting. An accomplished artist and designer, she could tackle any subject matter; however, she is most noted for her technique for painting realistic roses. The examples here showcase her extraordinary talent. Sadly, Joan passed away in 1990.

PEARS—PATTERN OF THE MONTH
Artist: Joan Johnson
Medium: Oil on mylar
Dimensions: 8-1/2 x 11 inches
(22 x 28 cm)

ANTIQUE TINWARE— PATTERN OF THE MONTH
Artist: Joan Johnson
Medium: Oil on mylar
Dimensions: 8-1/2 x 11 inches
(22 x 28 cm)

ROSES IN A STILL LIFE
Artist: Ann Kingslan
Medium: Oil on wood
Dimensions: 33-1/4 x 15-3/4
inches (84 x 40 cm)

OLD ENGLISH ROSES
Artist: Gloria Koskey
Medium: Oil on wood
Dimensions: 25 x 18 x 2 inches
(64 x 46 x 5 cm)

MY WISH
Artist: Izumi Kawamoto
Medium: Oil on wood
Dimensions: 16-1/2 x 9-3/4
inches (42 x 25 cm)

ROSES INSIDE AND OUT
Artist: Doxie Keller
Medium: Acrylic on wood
Dimensions: 14-1/2 x 25 x 9-1/4 inches
(38 x 64 x 24 cm)

TRAY
Artist: Per Lysne
Medium: Oil on wood
Dimensions: 21 x 14 inches (53 x 36 cm)

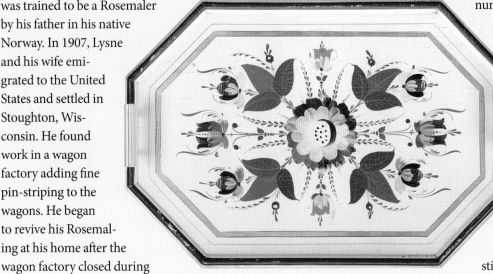

Per Lysne is credited with the introduction of Rosemaling into the United States. He was trained to be a Rosemaler by his father in his native Norway. In 1907, Lysne and his wife emigrated to the United States and settled in Stoughton, Wisconsin. He found work in a wagon factory adding fine pin-striping to the wagons. He began to revive his Rosemaling at his home after the wagon factory closed during the Depression. A commission to paint kitchen cabinets for actress Lynn Fontaine appeared in *Vogue* magazine and soon many other commissions followed. Lysne soon began to paint plates for the Marshall Fields catalogue.

Lysne's style of Rosemaling is unique to him and appears to be derived from a number of different styles of traditional Norwegian Rosemaling. He painted on white or ivory backgrounds, which was quite different from those of his homeland. Per Lysne passed away in 1947 but the tradition he brought to America still remains strong.

SMORGASBORD PLATE
Artist: Per Lysne
Medium: Oil on wood
Dimensions: 16 inches diameter
  (41 cm)

CUPBOARD
Artist: Peter Hunt
Medium: Enamel on wood
Dimensions: 45 x 69 x 18 inches (114 x 175 x 46 cm)

Peter Hunt was born Fredrick Schnitzer, but throughout his career claimed to be of royal descent. Hunt was an unforgettable character who charmed his way into high society circles. He is most noted for his brightly painted furniture and accessories. Hunt called his art "Transformagic." He would rescue castoff furniture and breathe new life into it by altering it and repainting it. His designs were based on Portuguese peasant paintings that he saw during World War I. Hunt often antiqued these pieces to add even more character to his work.

At the height of his popularity, Hunt's work was sold in major department stores across the country. He was also one of the first to write "How-To" books. After World War II he was so popular that in addition to his original pieces, he also designed decals, glassware, dishes and fabrics. Peter Hunt died in 1967. His work is highly sought after by folk art collectors and today his original pieces fetch record prices at auction. The cupboard pictured here is a glorious example of his work.

ROOSTER TRAY
Artist: Chesley Pearson
Medium: Oil on metal
Dimensions: 10 inches diameter (25 cm)

PETAL BY PETAL
Artist: Mary Jo Leisure
Medium: Oil on panel
Dimensions: 12 x 12 inches
(30 x 30 cm)

FAUX ROSES
Artist: Karl-Heinz Meschbach
Medium: Oil on wood
Dimensions: 14-1⁄4 x 13-3⁄4 x 6-3⁄4 inches
(36 x 35 x 17 cm)

WHITE ROSES
Artist: Pat Peniston
Medium: Oil on metal
Dimensions: 12 inches
diameter (30 cm)

BEYOND THE KEYS
Artist: June Varey
Medium: Mixed media on wood
Dimensions: 14 inches diameter
(36 cm)

PINK ROSE BOX
Artist: Dorothy Mullins
Medium: Oil on wood
Dimensions: 11-1⁄2 inches
diameter (29 cm)

CHIPPENDALE TRAY WITH FRUIT AND FLORAL DESIGN

Artist: Peter Ompir
Medium: Mixed media on metal
Dimensions: 19-1/2 x 25 inches
   (50 x 64 cm)

Charles Burns took the business name of Peter Ompir and became known as the "Dean of American Décor Painting." He was formally trained at the Art Institute of Chicago and at national and American art academies.

It was during the Depression that Ompir began to decorate castoff household items for resale. He decorated these objects with fruits, flowers and walking men in colonial garb. While these were the most popular subjects he painted, his repertoire was extensive in its diversity. It is interesting to note that many people believe that his paintings are from the 1800s. In fact, many of his pieces were painted in the late 20th century, but were painted on antiques.

The Decorative Arts Collection is pleased to have a sizable collection of Peter Ompir's work. His pieces were among the first that were purchased with funds made available from the Heart of Ohio Tole chapter of SDP.

PITCHER WITH ROOSTER AND TULIPS

Artist: Peter Ompir
Medium: Mixed media on metal
Dimensions: 8 inches high (20 cm)

DOLL CRADLE

Artist: Peter Ompir
Medium: Mixed media on wood
Dimensions: 4-3/4 x 10-1/2 x 4-1/2 inches
   (12 x 27 x 11 cm)

BREADBOARD WITH FRUIT
Artist: Peter Ompir
Medium: Mixed media on wood
Dimensions: 14 x 7 inches (36 x 18 cm)

**SCHOOLMASTER'S DESK WITH
STRAWBERRY BASKET**
Artist: Peter Ompir
Medium: Mixed media on wood
Dimensions: 16 x 25 x 24-1/2 inches
    (41 x 64 x 62 cm)

LANDSCAPE TRAY
Artist: Peter Ompir
Medium: Mixed media on metal
Dimensions: 12 inches diameter (30 cm)

**CLOCK SHELF WITH COLONIAL
MAN AND STRAWBERRY**
Artist: Peter Ompir
Medium: Mixed media on wood
Dimensions: 11 x 14 inches (28 x 36 cm)

FRUIT BOWL
Artist: Helen Roberts
Medium: Oil on wood
Dimensions: 11 x 15-1⁄2 x 4-1⁄4 inches
(28 x 39 x 11 cm)

ROSES FOR MOM
Artist: Heather Redick
Medium: Acrylics on wood
Dimensions: 28 x 22-3⁄4 inches
(71 x 58 cm)

FRAGRANT MEMORIES
Artist: Cheri Rol
Medium: Oil on panel
Dimensions: 13 x 15 inches (33 x 38 cm)

MOONLIGHT ROSE OF ZHOSTOVA

Artist: Jan Shaw
Medium: Oil on canvas
Dimensions: 29 x 25 inches
   (74 x 64 cm)

ROSEMALED BOWL

Artist: Claudine Schatz
Medium: Oil on wood
Dimensions: 15-1/2 inches
   diameter (39 cm)

STILL LIFE

Artist: Olav Okland
Medium: Oil on linen
Dimensions: 12 x 24 inches
   (30 x 61 cm)

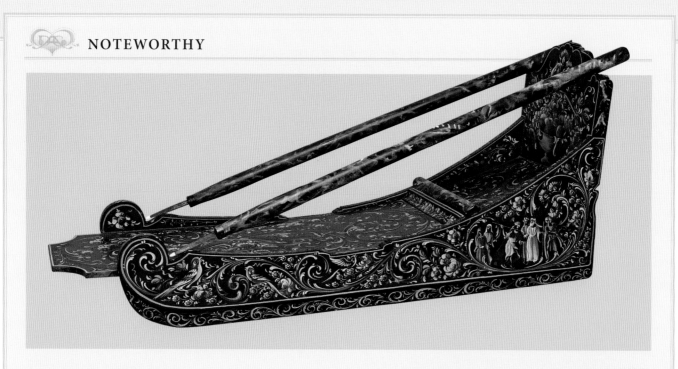

HINDELOOPEN SLED WITH MARBLEIZED PICKERS

Artist: Meine Visser
Medium: Oil on wood
Dimensions: 39 x 17-1/2 x 14 inches (99 x 44 x 36 cm)

This magnificent sled was painted by Meine Visser. It is a part of a collection of Hindeloopen pieces from the collection of Maud Oving of the Netherlands. This sled has many of the more familiar Hindeloopen motifs—scrolls, birds and stylized flowers. The sled also features biblical scenes on each side. The center of the sled is painted in a monochrome technique known as "porcelain technique." The sides and back are polychrome.

In older times a sled such as this, or larger, would have also been painted on the underside and when not in use, would have been hung in the house to add color to the sometimes drab interiors. The sled was propelled by the metal tipped "pickers" rather than being pulled. Note the stylized marbleizing technique used on the picker poles.

DETAIL OF INSIDE BACK OF
HINDELOOPEN SLED

DETAIL OF LONG SIDE OF
HINDELOOPEN SLED

CERAMIC JUG WITH APPLES
Artist: Werner C. Wrede
Medium: Mixed media on ceramic
Dimensions: 5-1/4 inches high (13 cm)

HARMONY
Artist: Zheniya Sivyakov
Medium: Egg tempera, gold on wood
Dimensions: 25-1/4 inches diameter (64 cm)

TIN BOX WITH WALKING MAN, BIRDS AND STROKEWORK
Artist: Werner C. Wrede
Medium: Mixed media on metal
Dimensions: 6-1/2 x 5 x 5 inches
        (17 x 13 x 13 cm)

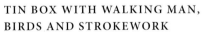

decorative arts collection awards

THE DECORATIVE ARTS COLLECTION AWARDS (DACA) is a juried art competition that showcases the best of the best of contemporary decorative painting. Entries and winners have come from all corners of the globe. The purchase awards for the Joan Johnson Award of Excellence and the 1st, 2nd, and 3rd place prizes allow us to increase the numbers of top quality pieces in the collection. The endless variety and consistent quality make the DAC Awards a prestigious competition. The winners are superb examples of the standard of contemporary decorative painting.

DONNA'S CAROUSEL
Artist: Della Nelson
Medium: Mixed media on wood
Dimensions: 14-1⁄4 inches diameter
   x 15 inches high (36 x 38 cm)
DACA 2nd Place winner 1993

BAVARIAN TRUNK
Artist: Naoko Seto
Medium: Acrylic on wood
Dimensions: 18 x 12 x 12-1⁄4 inches
   (46 x 30 x 31 cm)
DACA 1st Place winner 2000

CASA DE VINO
Artist: Lyly Souza De Guedikian
Medium: Acrylic on wood
Dimensions: 14 x 6 x 5 inches
   (36 x 15 x 13 cm)
DACA 1st Place winner 2001

HINDELOOPEN
Artist: Cheiko Nakano
Medium: Acrylic on metal
Dimensions: 9-1⁄2 x 6-3⁄4
   inches (50 x 17 cm)
*DACA 3rd Place winner
   2000*

LOTUS LAND
Artist: Michiko Kuroda
Medium: Acrylic on wood
Dimensions: 20 x 12 x 14 inches
   (51 x 30 x 36 cm)
DACA 2nd Place winner 2001

HOO'S THERE IN ZHOSTOVA
Artist: Slava Letkov
Medium: Oil on metal
Dimensions: 26 x 29 inches (66 x 74 cm)
DACA 3rd Place winner 2001

FIREWORKS ON A SUMMER NIGHT
Artist: Eriko Kaneko
Medium: Acrylic on wood
Dimensions: 20 x 15-1/2 inches (51 x 39 cm)
DACA 2nd Place winner 2002

ANTIQUE FLORAL
FANTASY
Artist: Toni McGuire
Medium: Acrylic on wood
Dimensions: 16-1⁄4 inches
   diameter (41 cm)
*DACA Joan Johnson Award
   of Excellence 2003*

HARMONY
Artist: Kumiko Watabe
Medium: Acrylic on wood
Dimensions: 29 x 22 inches (74 x 56 cm)
DACA 3rd Place winner 2002

CAT'S EYES
Artist: Ana Maria Bernabe
Medium: Acrylic on wood
Dimensions: 3-1⁄2 x 10-3⁄4 x 8
  inches (9 x 27 x 20 cm)
*DACA Joan Johnson Award of
  Excellence 2004*

BLUE IVY SUNDIAL
Artist: Naomi Shimanuki
Medium: Acrylic on wood
Dimensions: 34 x 34 inches
  (86 x 86 cm)
DACA 1st Place winner 2004

SHIP ON A STORMY SEA
Artist: Eriko Nakamura
Medium: Acrylic on wood
Dimensions: 10-1⁄2 x 17 x 18 inches
  (27 x 43 x 46 cm)
DACA 3rd Place winner 2003

SEAHORSES
Artist: Ana Bernabe
Medium: Acrylic on wood
Dimensions: 12 x 10 x 4 inches
  (30 x 25 x 10 cm)
DACA 1st Place winner 2005

COVERED PEDESTAL BOWL
Artist: Eldrid Arntzen
Medium: Oil on wood
Dimensions: 15 x 11-1/2 inches
  (38 x 29 cm)
DACA 3rd Place winner 1996

FANTASY
Artist: Karen Titus
Medium: Oil on wood
Dimensions: 19 inches diameter
  (23 cm)
DACA 2nd Place winner 1987

A RICHNESS OF ROSES
Artist: Priscilla Baldwin
Medium: Oil on glass
Dimensions: 12 x 6 inches each (30 x 15 cm)
DACA 3rd Place winner 2005

CELEBRATION TRAY
Artist: Hiromi Kida
Medium: Acrylic and mother-of-pearl
  on wood
Dimensions: 21-1/2 x 14 inches
  (55 x 36 cm)
DACA 1st Place winner 2003

index